BRESS
'N' NYAM

BRESS 'N' NYAM

Gullah Geechee Recipes from a Sixth-Generation Farmer

MATTHEW RAIFORD

with Amy Paige Condon

Photography by Siobhán Egan
Styling by Bevin Valentine Jalbert

The Countryman Press
A Division of W. W. Norton & Company
Independent Publishers Since 1923

Copyright © 2021 by CheFarmer Matthew Raiford and Amy Paige Condon
Photographs copyright © 2021 by Siobhán Egan and Bevin Valentine Jalbert

For information about permission to reproduce selections from this book, write to
Permissions, The Countryman Press, 500 Fifth Avenue, New York, NY 10110

For information about special discounts for bulk purchases, please contact
W. W. Norton Special Sales at specialsales@wwnorton.com or 800-233-4830

Manufacturing by RR Donnelley Asia Printing Solutions Limited
Book design by Allison Chi
Production manager: Devon Zahn

Library of Congress Cataloging-in-Publication Data

Names: Raiford, Matthew, author. | Condon, Amy Paige, author. | Egan,
Siobhán, illustrator. | Jalbert, Bevin Valentine, illustrator.
Title: Bress 'n' nyam : Gullah Geechee recipes from a sixth-generation
farmer / Matthew Raiford ; with Amy Paige Condon ; photography by
Siobhán Egan ; styling by Bevin Valentine Jalbert.
Description: New York, NY : The Countryman Press, a Division of
W. W. Norton & Company, Independent Publishers Since 1923, [2021] | Includes
bibliographical references and index.
Identifiers: LCCN 2020047976 | ISBN 9781682686041 | ISBN 9781682686058 (epub)
Subjects: LCSH: African American cooking. | Cooking, American—Southern
style. | Comfort food—Southern States. | LCGFT: Cookbooks.
Classification: LCC TX715.2.A47 R35 2021 | DDC 641.59/296073—dc23
LC record available at https://lccn.loc.gov/2020047976

The Countryman Press
www.countrymanpress.com

A division of W. W. Norton & Company, Inc.
500 Fifth Avenue, New York, NY 10110
www.wwnorton.com

978-1-68268-604-1

10 9 8 7 6 5 4 3 2 1

To my mother, Effie Holmes, who always said a recipe is not the rule but a guide.
Thank you for showing me how to smile and stand tall in the face of adversity.

To my father, Ulious Raiford, for showing me that although a zebra may not be able to change its
stripes, a man has the opportunity to make things right not by showing his hand but by his actions.

To my sestra, Althea Raiford, for being both my cheerleader and
the kick in the pants, often both at the same time.

And finally, to my Seven from Heaven—Shanelle, Kayla, Kenton, Kyra, Korvin,
Evan Amir, and Khloe—you all are the legacy. You are Jupiter's wildest dreams
come true and the reason I do this every day in the kitchen and on the farm.

The legacy is in the soil.

CONTENTS

Notes from a Prodigal Son

THERE ARE DAYS when I am standing in the fresh dirt just after the turmeric and ginger have gone into the ground and the chickens are making all kinds of fuss, and I just laugh that I am back here with a hoe in my hand. It's hardly picture-perfect—I'm not wearing a coiffed beard and Carhartt overalls surrounded by symmetrical rows of ruffled lettuces. There's a chicken coop to build as hurricane season fast approaches. (A few years ago, we learned never again to think "if" but "when," with three storms hitting within a 12-month period that destroyed our hoop house and beehives and uprooted every crop.) The compost heap needs attention, and the grass needs to be mowed. And there are so many seeds to plant. And it is so hot.

I knew it would be hard coming back. Not just the farming, but also as a Black man in the South who cooks in a kitchen and works the land. That's a lot of past to reckon with.

More than 30 years ago, at the age of 18, I stood right here and told my Nana, "I'm never coming back."

She looked me dead in the face and said, "Baby, you never know when you'll need to come home."

She was right. Nana was always right.

I am the great-great-great-grandson of Jupiter Gilliard, a descendant of the Tikar people of what is now Cameroon, a country sitting in the crook of equatorial Africa. Jupiter was born into slavery in South Carolina in 1812 and was sold or traded at some point before the Civil War to a landowner in Glynn County, Georgia. After emancipation, he began assembling property, most likely abandoned or sold off by white plantation owners afraid of slave revolt during the Reconstruction era. By 1870, Jupiter had amassed more than 450 acres 15 miles west of Brunswick, on which he paid nine dollars in taxes. Along with his wife Riner, a freedwoman from Florida, he broke this swampy, silty land; tilled the soil; planted seeds; sold the crookneck squash, field peas, corn, and cane syrup at market; and traded some with other Black farmers. For the first time in his life he could keep the money and raise a community. At the time of his death seven or eight years later, he had sold most of the land and passed on a little more than 40 acres to his sons.

One of those sons, London Gilliard, married Effie Short in 1881. On the farm, they raised Thomas, Arabella, and Florine, my great-grandmother. She married Horace Johnson in 1914, and on the land they built a deep-porched cottage to catch cross breezes just a few yards from a live oak tree that had been spreading its roots and limbs wide for more than a century before Jupiter even stepped foot on the soil. That house where Florine made hot buttermilk griddle cakes on an old wood-burning stove still stands today, although it is worse for wear and no longer in our hands—the parcel was sold off by a distant cousin who felt no kinship.

Florine gave birth to Effie Belle, Horace Jr., James, and Ophelia, in that order. Effie Belle was my maternal grandmother, but I never met her. She married Arthur Vickers, and they had two sons and a daughter. Arthur named the baby girl Effie Belle, in honor of his wife, who died during childbirth. Arthur left the farm, then moved to Opa-locka in Miami-Dade County, Florida. He took his two sons with him, but he left Effie Belle, my mother, in the care of her aunt Ophelia, who would forever become known to me as Nana.

Near the entrance gate to what is now Gilliard Farms, Jupiter had given an acre of land back to the county to build the Union School. It was the only schoolhouse for Black children in a 20-mile radius. They would walk through the woods or ride workhorses from all over just to study from history books that told them the Ku Klux Klan was simply a social fraternity that took on the role of keeping the Negro people in line from their "excesses." After the *Brown v. Board of Education* decision in 1954, the Union School closed. It's now a guesthouse, but every now and then, folks who remember going to school in that little green house will drive out to the farm and bring their children with them. I grew up with this history as my inheritance.

Nana graduated from Dorchester Academy, a liberal arts and industrial

Matthew Raiford's Family Tree

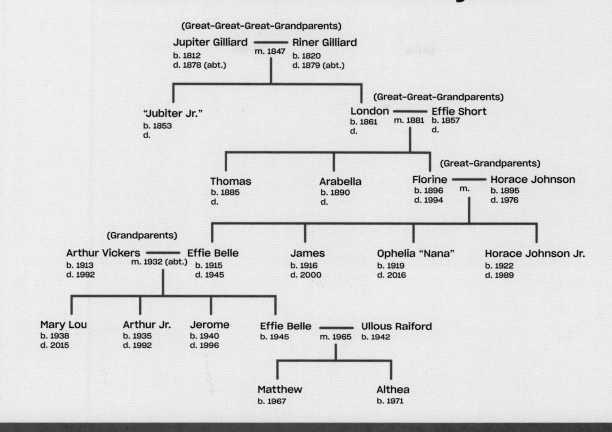

(Great-Great-Great-Grandparents)

Jupiter Gilliard
b. 1812
d. 1878 (abt.)

m. 1847

Riner Gilliard
b. 1820
d. 1879 (abt.)

"Jubiter Jr."
b. 1853
d.

(Great-Great-Grandparents)

London
b. 1861
d.

m. 1881

Effie Short
b. 1857
d.

Thomas
b. 1885
d.

Arabella
b. 1890
d.

(Great-Grandparents)

Florine
b. 1896
d. 1994

m.

Horace Johnson
b. 1895
d. 1976

(Grandparents)

Arthur Vickers
b. 1913
d. 1992

m. 1932 (abt.)

Effie Belle
b. 1915
d. 1945

James
b. 1916
d. 2000

Ophelia "Nana"
b. 1919
d. 2016

Horace Johnson Jr.
b. 1922
d. 1989

Mary Lou
b. 1938
d. 2015

Arthur Jr.
b. 1935
d. 1992

Jerome
b. 1940
d. 1996

Effie Belle
b. 1945

m. 1965

Ullous Raiford
b. 1942

Matthew
b. 1967

Althea
b. 1971

school established by the American Missionary Association just after the Civil War. She wanted to be a nurse, and she followed the Great Migration to Bridgeport, Connecticut. My mother went with her. During her years up North, Nana would write back and forth with her mother, Florine, keeping tabs on what was happening on the farm—what was growing, the weather— and the comings and goings of uncles and cousins, most of whom worked during the week for the Cottages at the Jekyll Island Club. Jekyll, one of many Sea Island resorts for the wealthy, was once inhabited by Saltwater Geechee, the descendants of enslaved people left to die on the barrier islands along the coast after white landowners abandoned their cotton, indigo, and rice plantations. Instead of dying, the Geechee thrived in collectives that shared their bountiful resources as well as their own language, music, art, and spiritual traditions. But without much understanding of land owner- ship and property rights, they found their wealth stripped, parcel by parcel.

While still in Connecticut, my mother married my father, Ulious Raiford, whose own family had fled North Carolina during the Great Migration seek- ing the promise of better schools, jobs, and less racism in the northeastern industrial cities. Those promises weren't always realized.

I came along in 1967. And, just before my little sister Althea was born, my mother and father packed us up and we moved to the farm, where Nana had returned many years before to care for her aging parents. She built a rambling, sort-of ranch house for herself, and we lived in the old house on the property that was once the Union School, amid an extended crew of aunts, uncles, and cousins. The farm was my sanctuary.

Even as a kid, I loved trailing after great-grandfather Horace, who was blind by this point but still knew his way around the farm, and my great- uncle, Horace Jr., as they knocked muscadines from the vines, picked wild blackberries by the side of the road, or pulled onions from the dirt. My favorite place was beside Nana and my mother and aunts in the kitchen as their hands stirred Gullah fish stew, peeled shrimp for creole, and spiced sweet potatoes for a pie.

Even then, I wanted to be a chef, but my daddy had other ideas. Back in Bridgeport, he'd worked in a bakery most of his adult life. He did not learn to read and write until he was 25 years old, but he could make the most delicate apple turnovers, tender-crumbed cakes, and shattering pie crusts you ever ate—yet he had never seen someone who looked like me or him as the head of a kitchen. Even though he was a pastry expert, when he and my mother migrated back to Brunswick in the early 1970s, he was denied jobs in bakeries. He was told flat out that he could not know more than his white bosses, and so he went to work as a boiler at the Lewis Crab Factory on Bay Street overlooking the East River, then finally as a long-shoreman at the port.

"A lot of things you can do, boy, but cooking ain't one of them," he said.

And so I graduated from high school and took the only road out of Brunswick that I could find. I went into the military with a new wife and baby in tow.

While we were stationed in Germany, I dove headfirst into trying new foods at Turkish restaurants and exploring different cooking techniques, but only as a hobby. As soon as my fellow soldiers learned I grew up in the South, however, they immediately mentioned how long it had been since they'd had a home-cooked meal. I loved throwing dinner parties for them where I could introduce my fellow servicemen and -women to the food of my people and of the Georgia coast.

From Germany, the US Army sent me to the Middle East, to Saudi Arabia, and along the way, I shopped the markets, cooked, and learned, still never believing that I could be a chef or that I would ever live again below the Mason-Dixon Line. Ten years later, after I completed my military career, I went to Howard University to study physiology. I was a 28-year-old fresh-man throwing parties and serving cathead biscuits, collard greens, and barbecue—and that's all I needed to set me back on the path to my origi-nal dream.

I dropped out of Howard and, in 1995, enrolled in a culinary program in Falls Church, Virginia. I still wasn't sure who I was as a chef or what my particular voice would be, but my teacher and mentor, Chef David Ivey-Soto, recognized that although I had an aptitude for the traditional French cooking techniques, my palate gravitated to the piquant and earthy season-ings and spices of Africa and the Caribbean.

As part of the program, I was invited to assist with Chef Joe Randall's annual Taste of Heritage dinner, and for the first time in my life I looked around a room and saw the representation I didn't know I craved—Leah Chase, Edna Lewis, Jessica B. Harris, Patrick Clark, all Black chefs and cookbook authors who spoke with pride of the rich heritage of African foodways as they sprang from the American South. It was the first time I began to understand that the food I grew up with wasn't a singular entity. It was the alchemy of Native American fires, Spanish conquest, Caribbean inflection, and West African ingenuity. These chefs, who looked like me, were doing some amazing work, and I knew that if I put in the effort, I could be there beside them. It was a moment I wish my father could have known.

Chef David encouraged me to enroll in the Culinary Institute of America in Hyde Park, and I graduated from the institute three years later. From there I went to Las Vegas, then Atlanta, then Washington, D.C. Later, I apprenticed at the University of California Santa Cruz's Center for Agroecology & Sustainable Food Systems, where I learned about seeds, organic pest control, and food justice—all things I knew from growing up but had never considered in an academic setting.

Then, in 2011, I returned to Gilliard Farms for a family reunion. The fields had grown weedy and fallow since my Nana and her brothers had aged beyond being able to care for them. My mom, my Aunt Mary Lou, my sister Althea, Nana, and I were sitting around the table talking about what to do with all the land. Nana had been smart and made sure the parcels that she had left were all in her name and the taxes were always up to date.

For years I had been telling Nana and my mom, "*Y'all* should go back to farming because that's what *y'all* know how to do."

But, during this conversation, I said, "*We* need to get back to farming."

My Nana reached under the table and handed my sister and me the deed to 28 of the remaining acres and said, "Well then, babies, *y'all* need to get to farming!"

I really believe that the ancestors just raised up inside of me at that moment. From the time I left home, I had never settled anywhere long enough to put down roots. So in 2011 I moved back to the farm for good. For a time, I served as the executive chef at the Lodge on Little St. Simons Island, threw down with Bobby Flay, collaborated with Alice Waters on the fiftieth anniversary of the agroecology program at Santa Cruz, opened (and closed) my own restaurant, and was named in 2017 a semifinalist for the James Beard award for the Best Chef of the Southeast.

I am a little bit of a "from-ya" and a "come-ya," meaning, in the Gullah Geechee context, someone from here and a visitor. But I am no longer passing through. I am the prodigal son who returned, only with my arms wide open for the land I thought I had left behind. Truth is, that old oak tree's roots held on and never let me go. These acres are producing again, and not just food. They serve as fertile ground to teach sustainable farming techniques, like planting sunn hemp as a cover crop to attract butterflies, dragonflies, and bees—the essential pollinator—and to keep deer away from tomatoes, corn, peppers, peas, and sweet potatoes. The muscadine vines planted by my great-grandfather, Horace, still bloom with plump grapes for jellies and sweets. The herb garden is filled with plants that Jovan Sage, my partner and a true food alchemist, uses to create shrubs, tinctures, and spice blends that she sells on her website and through our cooking classes at the farm.

I have plans for more: rice fields and hothouses will be built, and the sugarcane press given to my great-grandparents as a wedding present in 1919 will soon run again. The other day, my cousin's two-year-old son—the eighth generation of Jupiter Gilliard's family to live on this land—wanted me to show him a heel-toe method for planting peas. He was loving it, just like I did as a kid. He's learning where his food comes from, and that is important.

Not long ago, Jovan and I were going through dusty boxes stored in what was once my Nana's house—the home we live in now. I came across the letters Nana and Florine had written to each other when Nana lived in Connecticut. Florine's precise script is like an almanac for the farm. Tucked in one of those envelopes was a picture of Florine on Jekyll Island in 1938. In the box, also, was Jupiter Gilliard's grocery ledger and a Webster's Dictionary from 1898.

As I touch these vestiges of the past, I am reminded how those who came before me withstood the legal and social assaults of racism and discrimination by building self-sufficient communities. And I can't help but think that restaking our claim to these lands might help us to heal, to reconcile, to create a healthier way forward. Good food and good community go hand in hand. Maybe it's the key to resilience, and maybe now, we know our worth.

These yellow Norfolk sands and black river bottoms are as sacred to my kinfolk as the wild goldenrod that grows singular along the muddy banks of Igbo Landing on Dunbar Creek—the place where once-free West African tribesmen, chained together during the Middle Passage, walked into the brackish waters and drowned together rather than live enslaved. They are as hallowed as what is now St. Andrews Beach on the Jekyll River, where the last known slave ship, the *Wanderer*, landed more than 160 years ago. As sanctified as the ancient sand-and-clay loam beneath Gilliard Farms, where Freshwater Geechee, experts in irrigation, cultivated rice. This often unforgiving land is my home, and it has now fed my family for eight generations.

A cookbook can serve simply as a compendium of recipes or it can offer a story of a people and a place. I am the prodigal son, the custodian of Jupiter Gilliard's legacy. This book is my origin story.

In the words of the elders, "Bress 'n' Nyam."
Bless and eat, my friends.
CheFarmer Matthew Raiford

moderate oven (380° F.) for forty-five minutes. Cover with any desired icing.

CHOCOLATE NUT CAKE

⅔ cup butter or shortening
2 cups sugar
4 eggs
1 cup mashed potatoes
2 squares chocolate
2 cups flour
3½ teaspoons baking-powder

1 teaspoon cinnamon
½ teaspoon mace
½ teaspoon grated nutmeg
½ teaspoon ground cloves
1 cup chopped nut-meats
½ cup milk

Cream the butter or shortening and one cup of sugar. In another bowl, beat the egg-yolks with the remaining cup of sugar. Combine the two mixtures. Have ready the hot mashed potatoes, which should be without lumps, add to them the melted chocolate and combine with the first mixture. Mix and sift the dry ingredients and add the nut-meats. Add to the cake mixture, alternating with the milk. Fold in the stiffly beaten whites. Bake in a loaf pan in a moderate oven (380° F.). When cool, cover with marshmallow frosting or boiled frosting. This is a large moist cake, which will keep well.

CHOCOLATE LOAF CAKE

2 tablespoons butter or shortening
1 cup sugar
2 tablespoons grated chocolate
2 cups flour

2 teaspoons baking-powder
1 cup milk
2 cups seeded raisins
12 black walnut-meats
½ teaspoon vanilla extract

Cream the butter or shortening; add the sugar and continue creaming. Melt the chocolate over hot water, and add. Mix and sift the flour and baking-powder and add alternately with the milk. Add the raisins, broken nut-meats well floured, and the flavoring. Mix well. Bake in a loaf pan 360° F. for forty-five minutes. When cool, frost with boiled or chocolate frosting.

CHOCOLATE SOUR-MILK CAKE

½ cup butter or shortening
1 cup sugar
3 eggs
½ cup sour milk

2 cups flour
⅓ teaspoon soda
⅓ cup hot water
1 square chocolate

with the milk. Stir in the chopped nut-meats and add the flavoring. Fold in the stiffly beaten egg-whites. Bake in layer-cake tins in a moderate oven (380° F.) for forty-five minutes. When cold, spread chocolate frosting between layers and on top.

NUT CAKE

½ cup butter or shortening
1 cup sugar
2 cups flour

2 teaspoons baking-powder
¾ cup milk
1 cup chopped nut-meats
4 egg-whites

Cream butter or shortening and add the sugar. Mix and sift the dry ingredients and add alternately with the milk. Add nut-meats, well floured, and fold in the egg-whites. Bake in a square loaf pan at 380° F., and frost the top when cool, using any desired icing.

GOLDEN CAKE

¼ cup butter or shortening
½ cup sugar
3 egg-yolks
1 cup flour

2 teaspoons baking-powder
¼ cup milk
1 teaspoon orange extract

Cream the butter or shortening and add the sugar gradually. Beat the yolks until thick and lemon-colored. Mix and sift the dry ingredients and add to the first mixture alternately with the milk. Flavor. Bake as loaf or layer cake, in a moderate oven (380° F.) for forty-five minutes.

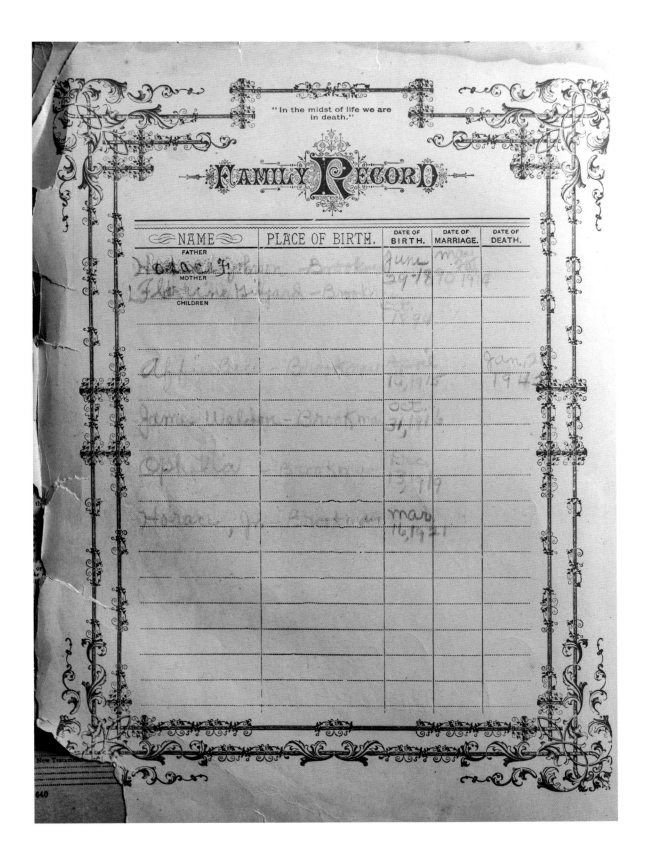

"In the midst of life we are
in death."

FAMILY RECORD

NAME	PLACE OF BIRTH.	DATE OF BIRTH.	DATE OF MARRIAGE.	DATE OF DEATH.
FATHER				
Horace Finklin	Brooklyn	June 29, 1870	May 3rd 1914	
MOTHER				
2 Florence Gifford – Brooklyn		Feb. 1894		
CHILDREN				
Affie Belle	Blackwood	April 16, 1918		Jan. 1947
James Weldon – Brooklyn		Oct. 31, 1916		
Ophelia	Brooklyn	Dec. 13, 1919		
Horace J.	Brooklyn	Mar. 16, 1921		

About This Book

IT IS TRADITION among the Gullah Geechee that when we need answers, we turn to the wisdom of the ancestors, our source. And just as I returned to my source, Gilliard Farms, to follow my life's calling, I have organized the recipes in this book according to their elemental beginnings: earth, water, fire, wind, nectar, and spirits. Within each of the chapters, recipes are loosely grouped according to ingredients, whether they be grains or greens, shellfish or mollusks, pork or beef, rum or bourbon. Within the recipes and headnotes, you will find recommendations for recipe pairings to help with meal planning.

As an observer of Kwanzaa, I strive to live daily by its principles—unity, self-determination, collective work and responsibility, cooperative economics, purpose, creativity, and faith. This book is not just about me and my journey. It's about all the people who brought me to this moment, from family to fellow chefs and growers. To lift up and honor the good work of people in our region who work hard daily to harvest wholesome, organic food, who honor animals through humane practices, and who nourish not just our bodies but our minds and spirits, I have noted within the recipes where I have used their peas, syrups, rice, and grits. Plus, I have provided a resource section so that you can seek out these purveyors and handmake a dish that is as authentic to the vision of this book as possible.

Eart / Earth

When I returned to Gilliard Farms in 2011, I was full of ambition. I had been to Hyde Park! I had studied sustainable food systems in California! I wanted to re-create rice fields in two depressions beneath a canopy of oaks and seed them with the robust heirloom grains once cultivated by my great-great-great-grandfather Jupiter. I envisioned bountiful rows of tomatoes, squash, corn, peppers, peas, sweet potatoes, and watermelons.

Nana watched as I tilled that fallow, silty soil in preparation for late spring plantings. Up popped nutsedge—the most unforgiving weed—then scarlet runner and coffeeweed. All those seeds raised from the soil to feed off the sun and rain after years of lying dormant in the earth. They went wild!

Then I planted fruit trees, thinking I'd revive the orchards. I toured Nana through all of my back-breaking work.

Leaning on the broken broomstick she used as a cane, she pointed to one tree, "W'at dat is?"

"Apple," I said. And it went on like that row by row. Every time I answered, she raised a brow. When we got to the fig sapling, she said, "Tell me when that come in."

Every tree, except the fig, died, and I thought, Nana done put a hex on things. Really, it was me not knowing what I didn't know. She would tease me that I had gone and got a degree in everything she had already taught me.

That's when Nana gave me the keys to the kingdom, pulling out old letters, dating as far back as the 1940s and stashed away in boxes, that detailed what was planted and when. What worked. What didn't. The weather. Together, these letters and Nana's advice are my lodestar.

Now we grow ginger and turmeric—some of the original crops cultivated by General James Oglethorpe in 1733 at the Trustees' Garden in Savannah, Georgia, the first city in the state. We have hibiscus for teas and shrubs, and we have Sea Island Red Peas for Reezy-Peezy (page 38) and fritters. We've harvested tomatoes for jams and pizzas, and strawberries for ice cream. Soon there will be greens to stew and ladle atop grits, and we'll have herbs for tinctures, kombucha, and spice blends to season our dishes, instead of salt.

And that little fig tree? Despite an overzealous mower that cut it down in its youth, it's growing again, soon to bear fruit.

CheFarmer's Grits

Basic grits require only four ingredients: water, grits, salt, and pepper. They are cooked low and slow until they alchemize into a creamy porridge that is fabulous morning, noon, or night. The quality of your grits matters, and I suggest investing in either Geechie Boy Mill or Anson Mills brands, because they both rely on heirloom grains and old-world production methods. I do, however, add some special ingredients when I want to push my grits over the top as a side to Smokin' Hot 'n' Sweet Shrimp and Grits with Vidalia Onion Sausage (page 106) or with a Mess o' Greens (page 56).

SERVES 4 TO 6

3 cups water, more if needed

1 teaspoon kosher salt

1 cup stone-ground grits

½ cup buttermilk

½ cup heavy cream, more if needed

1 tablespoon unsalted butter

1 tablespoon pecan oil

IN A HEAVY-BOTTOMED medium stockpot, bring the water with the salt to a boil. Add the grits and stir, bringing them back to a boil.

AS THE GRITS begin to thicken, add the buttermilk and cream, then reduce the heat to a simmer, stirring occasionally for 45 minutes until the grits are creamy and thick. If the grits start to thicken quickly, add equal parts water and cream. Stir in the butter and oil just before serving.

Saffron and Coconut Milk Rice

This sunny, delicate, and fragrant rice dish can serve as a flavorful side dish for the Calypso Pork Loin (page 130) or the Snapper on the Half Shell (page 91). Because of its light floral notes and natural sweetness, this rice dish can serve as a gluten- and dairy-free decadence for people with food allergies. I prefer this rice as a one-pot savory dish, served with roasted vegetables and seasoned with white pepper and pink Himalayan salt. For a sweeter version, stir in 1 cup chopped fresh mango or pineapple.

SERVES 4 TO 6

One 13.5-ounce can coconut milk

1½ cups warm water

10 saffron threads

2 teaspoons pink Himalayan salt

3 cups white rice

½ teaspoon white pepper

IN A MEDIUM saucepan over high heat, stir together the coconut milk and water. Add the saffron threads and salt, then bring the liquid to a boil.

ADD THE RICE and turn the heat down to a simmer, allowing the rice to cook for 20 minutes. Check to ensure all the liquid is absorbed before removing the rice from the heat. Sprinkle with the white pepper and fluff with a fork before serving.

NOTE: *Saffron comes from the crocus plant and is found throughout the Middle East and Mediterranean. I began cooking with it when I served overseas during Operation Desert Storm.*

Did You Know?

Pink Himalayan salt, pulled in blocks from the foothills of the Himalayas on the border between India and Pakistan, is considered the purest salt on earth. Its rosy hue speaks to its wealth of trace minerals, including natural iodine. Its intense zest means you can use less of it in a dish and still heighten the flavors of meats and vegetables.

Rice as the Foundation

Beginning in the 18th century, rice, specifically an ancient variety of gold rice, served as the cash crop of the tidewater communities along the coasts of the Carolinas and Georgia, what is now the heart of the Gullah Geechee Cultural Heritage Corridor. When enslaved West Africans from rice cultivation areas along the Niger River watershed and the coastline of equatorial Africa were brought to the Americas through ports in Sullivan's Island, Savannah, and New Orleans, they brought with them grains and seeds, plus the know-how to level land and create irrigation ditches with systems of gates to manage water flow through saltwater marshes and freshwater swamps. The rice first served as subsistence food for our enslaved ancestors, then became a valuable commodity for plantation owners. *The Darien Journal of John Girardeau Legare, Ricegrower* (UGA Press, 2010) presents a detailed record of the rise and fall of rice growing just after the Civil War.

The resilience of rice reflected the strength of the people who, when abandoned and left to die on the Sea Islands after the Civil War, instead thrived and maintained a language and other cultural traditions, like call-and-response shout singing, oral storytelling, and intricate arts like crab net tying and sweetgrass basket making, which also had the practical purpose of easing some of the brutal work. And this is why rice, not potatoes, is the foundation of Lowcountry and coastal one-pot cookery, from richly layered gumbos to creoles, jambalayas, and purloos (or perloos). These dishes speak to where you came up, who your people are—from the mainland or the ocean, near the city or in the country.

Gullah Rice

This one-pot dish is akin to a purloo or a jambalaya. It evokes the traditional tomato-based Savannah Red Rice but is steeped in a hearty vegetable stock. When I was coming up, a bowl of rice with some roasted vegetables in it was often dinner, especially when meat proved scarce. I still find it comforting, just as I did during those lean years when I was at Howard University, right after getting out of the Army. Anytime someone would say they didn't have any food in the house, I would invite folk over and serve my version of Gullah Rice, finished with a handful of fresh arugula that wilts lightly from the heat.

SERVES 4

1 cup red onion, roughly chopped

4 tablespoons bacon grease or butter

1 bell pepper, roughly chopped

2 cloves garlic, smashed and roughly chopped

1 teaspoon smoked paprika

1 teaspoon pink Himalayan salt

1 whole habanero pepper

One 28-ounce can crushed tomatoes

1¾ cups Vegetable Stock (recipe follows)

1 cup Carolina Gold Rice or another long-grain rice

IN A DEEP skillet or Dutch oven over medium-high heat, sauté the onion in the bacon grease until it starts to soften, approximately 3 to 4 minutes, then add the bell pepper and sauté for another minute or two more.

TOSS IN THE garlic, paprika, salt, and habanero pepper. Pour in the crushed tomatoes and vegetable stock, then let the vegetable mixture come to boil.

STIR IN THE rice and turn the heat down to a simmer and cover. Every 5 minutes or so over a 20-minute period, stir the rice until all the liquid is absorbed. Remove the rice from the heat, taste and add a pinch or two more of salt to your liking. Allow the rice to rest for 5 minutes before serving.

TIP: *If you want to add meat, sauté sliced smoked or andouille sausage, or chicken tenders cut into chunks, for 5 to 7 minutes before adding the onion. For shrimp, add peeled and deveined shrimp during the last 5 minutes of cooking.*

(CONTINUED)

Vegetable Stock

2 quarts water

1 pound yellow onions, roughly chopped (do not use sweet onions)

½ pound baby bella mushrooms, roughly chopped

½ pound carrots, roughly chopped

2 stalks celery, roughly chopped

1 tablespoon sea salt

1 sprig rosemary

1 sprig thyme

1 sprig oregano

2 cloves garlic, smashed

PLACE ALL THE ingredients in a large stockpot over high heat and bring to a roaring boil. Turn the heat to low and let the stock simmer for 1 hour.

REMOVE THE STOCK from the heat and let it cool to room temperature. Once cooled, strain the stock into 2-cup portions in sealable containers and place in the refrigerator, where it will keep up to 2 weeks. In the freezer, the stock will keep up to 6 months.

TIP: *Make a double or triple batch of this stock to keep on hand for rice dishes, soups, and sautés. You can freeze it or keep it refrigerated for up to two weeks. You may add clippings from other vegetables, such as asparagus and other greens, for added flavor, depth, and nutrients. Throw any of your leftover vegetable peels into your compost bin.*

Reezy-Peezy

Most folks know about Hoppin' John, the fabled New Year's Day dish on many a Southern table. That dish, just like the song "Kumbaya," has its origins among the Gullah Geechee, who planted the peas and rice as subsistence food from beans and seeds carried with them from Africa. We call it Reezy-Peezy and make it year-round. It's hearty enough to serve as a main dish. Or serve over a bowl of Jupiter Brown Rice.

SERVES 6 TO 8

1¼ pounds Sea Island Red Peas, covered with water and soaked overnight in the refrigerator

1 gallon water

1 yellow onion, peeled, cut through root end with layers left intact

1 carrot, peeled and roughly chopped

2 small inner celery ribs, leaves attached, roughly chopped

2 garlic cloves, peeled

1 small Turkish bay leaf

1½ teaspoons curry powder

A healthy pinch of red pepper flakes

1 teaspoon fine sea salt

½ teaspoon freshly ground black pepper

DRAIN THE PEAS and set aside. In a large, heavy-bottomed stockpot, bring the water to a simmer over medium-high heat.

STIR IN THE peas, onion, carrot, celery, garlic, bay leaf, and curry powder. Return the liquid to a simmer, and then reduce the heat to low. Cover the pan partially and simmer gently, stirring occasionally, until the peas are tender, approximately 60 to 90 minutes.

REMOVE AND DISCARD the vegetables and bay leaf. Season with the red pepper flakes and salt to taste. Remove 4 cups of peas and broth and puree them in a separate bowl with an immersion blender. Return the puree to the pot with the peas (alternately, you can mash a quarter of the peas in the pot with a potato masher).

IF THE GRAVY is too thick, thin it with a bit of warm water or vegetable stock. Then cook again until just heated through. Taste for seasoning.

VARIATION

Sea Island Red-Peas-and-Rice Fritter

If you have any leftover Reezy-Peezy, serve it as a fritter or as a veggie burger. This fritter is modeled after *akara* (a Yoruban word), a pea fritter common in Ghana and Nigeria.

SERVES 8

1 batch of Reezy-Peezy (above, without additional liquid)
2 cups cooked long-grain rice, such as Carolina Gold Rice
2 eggs, beaten
2 cups panko bread crumbs (use gluten-free, if necessary)
Vegetable oil

IN A LARGE bowl, combine the Reezy-Peezy, rice, and eggs until thick and able to shape into patties.

PLACE THE BREAD crumbs on a plate. Using a regular ice cream scoop or large serving spoon, scoop the pea and rice mixture, shape into patties, and lightly coat with bread crumbs.

IN A LARGE nonstick skillet, heat 2 teaspoons vegetable oil on medium-high. Once the oil is hot enough that a drop of water sizzles, lay the patties into the hot pan, in batches of three or four without touching, and cook 3 to 4 minutes per side, or until golden brown. Serve immediately.

Cowpea Salad

The black-eyed pea, also known as the cowpea or crowder pea, was indigenous to the semiarid regions of Nigeria and Ghana. Even though it often was used to feed livestock, it provided sustenance to poor farmers, and it is proof positive that you can make just about anything delicious with the right blend of ingredients. This fresh, tart salad provides a cool brightness to potluck suppers and summer cookouts.

SERVES 8 TO 10

6 cups cooked cowpeas

½ cup diced Vidalia or other sweet onion

2 mangoes, peeled and finely diced

1 orange bell pepper, finely diced

1 small bunch cilantro, no stems, roughly chopped

½ cup lime juice

½ cup olive oil

2 teaspoons sea salt

½ teaspoon freshly cracked pepper

3 scallions, sliced on the bias

½ pound arugula

IN A LARGE bowl, combine the cowpeas, onions, mangoes, bell pepper, and cilantro, and stir until mixed well.

IN A SMALL bowl, whisk together the lime juice, olive oil, salt, and pepper until just combined. Pour the lime dressing over the cowpeas and toss until incorporated. Taste and adjust the seasoning as needed.

DIVIDE THE SCALLIONS and arugula on salad plates, then spoon the pea mixture evenly across the arugula and serve.

Lesson Learned

Just after I left UC Santa Cruz and returned to the farm, I did everything I could to amend the soil so that I could plant my own Sea Island red peas. But my plantings grew into these lush, beautiful bushes with no peas at all. So I went to the source, Miss Cornelia Walker Bailey, the late Geechee historian and storyteller of Hog Hammock, who was born and lived all her life on Sapelo Island. She laughed with me as I told her the story of how I planted my peas. Miss Cornelia then showed me her heel-toe method for how to drop a pea into the sandy loam and lightly cover it, then leave it alone. Like Nana often did, Miss Cornelia reminded me that I was overthinking it.

Basic Beer Bread with Whipped Feta

While craft brews are all the rage these days, Georgia was ahead of the trend as far back as 1743. General James Oglethorpe appointed Major William Horton to the command at Fort Frederica on St. Simons Island. For his service, Horton received 500 acres on the north end of Jekyll Island to establish a farm to feed the troops at the fort. Horton also grew hops and barley for ale to quench their thirst. (Hard liquor was outlawed—along with lawyers and slavery. None of these prohibitions lasted long.) More than 275 years later, the tabby walls of Horton House still stand. The few remaining ruins of the brewery sit just down the road from the homestead on DuBignon Creek. This bread is inspired by the coast's long history with craft beer. You can also serve this bread with Sweet Potato and Red Pepper Soup (page 71).

SERVES 4 TO 6

Butter for pan

3 cups self-rising flour, sifted

½ teaspoon fine sea salt

6 teaspoons freshly ground black pepper

12 ounces beer, preferably an IPA

Whipped Feta (recipe follows)

BUTTER A SMALL loaf pan and set aside. Preheat the oven to 375°F.

IN A LARGE bowl, gently mix together the flour, salt, and pepper. Make a well in the middle, then pour in the beer. Stir gently with a fork until you have a sticky dough. Turn the dough onto a lightly floured surface and form the dough into a loaf.

PLACE THE DOUGH into the loaf pan and let it sit for 10 minutes before baking the bread in the preheated oven for 20 to 25 minutes. Rotate the pan a half turn, then bake for 20 minutes more, until crisp and golden brown.

SKEWER FOR DONENESS. Let rest a few minutes, then slice and serve with Whipped Feta.

(CONTINUED)

VARIATIONS

Garlic Beer Bread

ADD 4 TABLESPOONS fresh garlic, minced.

Cheesy Beer Bread

ADD 1 CUP freshly grated white Cheddar, pepper Jack, or your favorite mixture of hard cheeses. You could also add the garlic from the variation above and make it Cheesy Garlic Beer Bread.

Sweet Beer Bread

ADD 1 CUP semisweet chocolate chips and use Breckenridge Brewery's Vanilla Porter for the beer. This version is great toasted and served with ice cream.

Whipped Feta

MAKES 2 CUPS

8 ounces feta cheese

8 ounces goat cheese

8 ounces organic cream cheese

1 teaspoon pink Himalayan salt

1 teaspoon cracked black pepper

IN A FOOD processor, whip together the cheeses until they are airy and smooth. Spoon into a medium bowl, sprinkle with the salt and pepper, then serve with toasted slices of beer bread.

Hot Buttermilk Biscuits with Honey Butter

I don't really go out and buy buttermilk. My Nana taught me how to make it myself, and I still do it that way: 2 to 3 teaspoons of fresh-squeezed lemon juice for every 1 cup of room-temperature heavy cream. But feel free to save some time and purchase a good quality buttermilk. When it comes to flour, I've got people who swear that White Lily self-rising flour is the only flour for biscuits in the South. I use King Arthur brand, but use whichever one you're most loyal to.

MAKES 12 BISCUITS

2¼ cups self-rising flour

¼ teaspoon (a pinch) of fine sea salt

1½ cups buttermilk

Honey Butter (recipe follows)

PREHEAT THE OVEN to 375°F and line a baking sheet with parchment paper.

COMBINE 2 CUPS of the flour and the salt in a bowl. Add the buttermilk to the flour mixture and stir until the dough starts to take on a tacky consistency (where the dough barely sticks to your palm when you lay it on top of the dough).

USING HALF OF the remaining flour, dust the countertop and turn the biscuit dough onto the floured surface. Using a rolling pin, roll out the dough to a half-inch thickness, and fold over twice. Repeat twice, then roll the dough to a half-inch thick.

DIP A MEDIUM-SIZED biscuit cutter into the remaining flour, shake off the excess, then punch out biscuits from the dough (do not twist or turn the cutter). Place the biscuits on the prepared baking sheet. Put the baking sheet in the oven and bake the biscuits for 12 to 15 minutes, until the biscuits are golden brown. Serve warm with Honey Butter.

(CONTINUED)

Sweet Cream

THE BASIC BISCUIT dough is versatile and can be adapted for a sweeter, less tangy version that can be used as a dumpling in the Blackberry Doobie (page 194) or rolled into the Strudel with Almost Rum Syrup (page 192). Simply substitute heavy cream for the buttermilk and increase the salt to ½ teaspoon.

Honey Butter

MAKES 1 CUP

¼ cup locally sourced wildflower honey

1 cup unsalted butter

Pinch of kosher salt

PLACE THE HONEY and butter in a small pan and warm it over low heat until the butter just melts. Remove the pan from the stove and allow the butter to cool for 10 minutes. Add a pinch of salt.

USING AN IMMERSION blender, puree the honey mixture until the honey and butter combine and the color turns slightly lighter than the original honey color. Pour the butter into a pint-sized mason jar and seal. Store in the refrigerator for up to 1 month.

Naan

It's not as if Brunswick, Georgia, was full of ethnic restaurants as I was coming up. So I did not try naan, the traditional Persian flatbread, until I served in Germany and went to a Turkish restaurant. I loved this bread's versatility—and as a vehicle for hummus, a simple and portable snack. As I traveled, it dawned on me how versions of flatbreads showed up in different cooking traditions, from Asia to Africa to southern Europe, reinforcing for me how food is not only an amalgam of the hands from the many nations that make and serve it, but how it also is a form of communion unto itself. That's why this easy, adaptable, imperfect bread is an essential dish in my kitchen.

MAKES 12 ROUNDS

2½ cups all-purpose flour

2½ cups whole wheat flour

3 teaspoons rapid rise yeast

1 tablespoon kosher salt

1 tablespoon extra virgin olive oil

1 cup warm water

COMBINE THE FLOURS, yeast, and salt in a medium mixing bowl. In a separate and larger bowl, whisk together the oil and water.

GRADUALLY ADD ABOUT half of the flour to the liquids and mix until the dough is stiff. Knead in the remaining flour until all the flour is incorporated. Cover the bowl with a clean towel and leave in a warm place for 30 minutes until it has rested and doubled.

IN THE BOWL, knead the dough again for about 10 minutes or until the dough is smooth to the touch. Allow the dough to rest for an additional 30 minutes or until it has doubled in size.

DIVIDE THE DOUGH into a dozen equal pieces, then let rest for another 15 minutes. While the dough rests, prepare your baking source.

THERE ARE VARIOUS ways to bake this bread to your liking: Preheat an oven to 450°F and place a small dish of water on the bottom rack. Or rub a grill with expeller-pressed canola, grape-seed, or other high–smoke-point oil and heat it to at least 450°F, or set a cast-iron skillet on medium-high heat and melt 2 teaspoons of ghee or clarified butter.

RETURN TO THE dough and flatten each piece, rolling each one into a small round, about ¼ inch thick. Keep the rolls covered until all the rounds are ready to bake.

IN THE OVEN: Place a nonstick baking sheet or a slightly oiled baking sheet in the oven for 3 minutes. Remove the sheet and place three rounds on the sheet and bake for 3 minutes. Brush olive oil on the top.

ON THE GRILL: Set the rounds on the grill surface and cook 1 to 2 minutes per side, brushing the tops with a little olive oil.

IN THE SKILLET: Place a round in the hot skillet and brush the top with ghee or clarified butter. Once the round begins to lift up, flip it and let it slightly char on the edges, about 1 to 2 minutes per side.

TIP: *For an easy pizza, spread the naan with Tomato Jam (page 148) and your favorite vegetables, meats, and cheeses, then grill, covered, for 3 minutes.*

Buttermilk Griddle Cakes with Muscadine Jelly

My great-grandmother Florine, who lived in a wood-sided cottage on the farm until she was 100 years old, used to make these cornmeal pancakes (what most folk call hoecakes) right on the big, round top burners of an old potbellied stove that sat across from the piano my Nana played. I still have one of her old irons that I use as a doorstop. Slathered in butter and Muscadine Jelly, the griddle cakes were our after-school snack—our version of a peanut butter and jelly sandwich.

MAKES 12 PANCAKES

1 cup yellow cornmeal

2 cups self-rising flour

1 teaspoon pink Himalayan or kosher salt

3 large eggs

3 tablespoons salted butter, melted

1 cup buttermilk, store-bought or homemade

1 tablespoon locally sourced honey

Clarified unsalted butter or ghee, melted

Muscadine Jelly (recipe follows)

PREHEAT THE OVEN to 200°F. Line a baking sheet with parchment paper.

COMBINE THE CORNMEAL, flour, and salt in a large bowl and create a well in the center. In a separate bowl, whisk together the eggs, the salted butter, buttermilk, and honey. Pour the wet ingredients into the well of the dry ingredients and whisk together until just incorporated and no lumps are left. Let batter sit for 10 minutes.

PLACE A CAST-IRON skillet over medium heat for 2 minutes, then pour in a tablespoon of the clarified butter to coat the bottom of the pan.

USING A REGULAR-SIZED ice cream scoop or ladle, spoon 2 to 3 griddle cakes into the hot skillet, making sure not to crowd the pan. Allow each cake to cook 1 minute, or until the edges appear dry. Then, using a long and broad spatula, flip each cake over. Cook until golden brown, about 1 minute more.

REMOVE THE CAKES from the pan and place on the prepared baking sheet in the preheated oven to keep warm as you cook the rest of the griddle cakes. Serve warm with butter and Muscadine Jelly or Muscadine Compote.

(CONTINUED)

My great-grandfather Horace found wild-growing vines of muscadine grapes in the woods around the farm and replanted them in an arbor near the fields. In early fall, around the end of September, Nana would take her all-purpose broomstick handle—the one she used as a walking cane, a fire stoker, and a whooping stick for unruly children—and tap the vines. If the grapes held, she'd say they weren't ready. If one or two grapes fell, we would take clean, bleached white sheets and spread them all under the arbor and thrash the vines until all those bronzed and rose-gold globes had fallen. Some were used to make wine, others for jellies, jams, and compotes. Making the jelly is a two-day process, and you'll need canning jars and a large stockpot to make it. If you don't have two days, try the short, simple, and sweet recipe for Muscadine Compote (page 54) as a substitute.

Muscadine Jelly

**MAKES 8 TO 10
HALF-PINT JARS**

4 quarts muscadine grapes

3 cups unchlorinated water
(well or tap water that
has been sitting out for at
least 24 hours)

8 tablespoons powdered
no-sugar pectin

1 tablespoon fresh lime juice

5 cups sugar

DAY ONE

PLACE THE MUSCADINES and water into a large stockpot and bring to a boil over medium-high heat. Turn down to low and simmer until the skins of the muscadines split open.

REMOVE THE POT from the heat. Using a potato masher, press the grapes to release all their juices, then strain the grapes through a sieve into a large (8-cup) measuring cup or bowl. Set aside and cool to room temperature, then place in the refrigerator, covered, for 24 hours.

DAY TWO

STRAIN THE COOLED muscadine juice through cheesecloth into a large stockpot. You want to ensure there are no solids in the juice.

PREP YOUR CANNING jars and lids according to the manufacturer's instructions or by running them through the sanitize cycle of your dishwasher.

MEANWHILE, MIX THE pectin with the muscadine and lime juice in the stockpot and bring to a boil over medium-high heat, stirring occasionally. Once the pectin has fully dissolved, start pouring in the sugar, stirring constantly. Bring the jelly back to a boil.

LET THE JELLY boil hard for 1 minute, stirring constantly. Remove from the heat, then using a wooden spoon, skim off the frothy foam. Ladle or pour the jelly, evenly distributing among the sterilized jars, leaving a ¼-inch space at the top of each jar.

PLACE THE LIDS on the jars and screw down tightly. Wipe any excess jelly off the jars. Following the manufacturer's instructions, place the jars into the canner and boil for 5 minutes. Remove

(CONTINUED)

the jars from the canner and let cool to room temperature. The jelly can be stored in a cool dry place for up to 1 year, but once the jars are opened, they will need to be stored in the refrigerator for up to 2 weeks.

TIP: *When muscadines are not in season, substitute 1 pound each of calamondins and kumquats, roughly chopped, and replace the lime juice with Meyer lemon juice.*

VARIATION
Muscadine Compote

Not up for a two-day process? Here's a quick and easy variation.

4 cups muscadine grapes
1 cup water
¼ cup white wine vinegar
¼ cup sweet onion, finely diced
2 tablespoons locally sourced honey
Pinch of kosher salt

TAKE 1 CUP of the grapes and cut them in half. With a sharp paring knife, remove all the seeds while preserving much of the gelatinous grape part in place.

PLACE THE REMAINING 3 cups of grapes in a heavy-bottomed stockpot with the water and bring to a roaring boil, then turn down to a simmer for 10 minutes. Using the back of a wooden spoon, mash the grapes into a chunky mixture and cook for an additional 5 minutes.

USING A STRAINER double-lined with clean cheesecloth, strain the mashed grapes. Reserve the skin and seeds for composting.

POUR THE STRAINED juice back into the stockpot and add the halved muscadine grapes, vinegar, onions, and honey and bring to a simmer for about 5 minutes, stirring occasionally.

TASTE THE COMPOTE and adjust sweetness by adding a pinch of salt.

Mess o' Greens

My Aunt Mary Lou used to make what she called a "mess of greens," and I couldn't get enough of them. But it wasn't until I traveled in the military that I learned people either (1) had no idea what collards were, (2) had eaten badly cooked greens, which turned them off of them forever, or (3) were too intimidated to cook them. Greens can be temperamental: pulled too soon from the stove, they can be tough and spiky; pulled too late, they can be a soupy, mushy mess. I love these greens ladled over a bowl of CheFarmer's Grits (page 29) or as a side to Za'atar Roasted Chicken (page 155).

SERVES 4 TO 6

2 tablespoons olive oil

2 medium yellow onions, peeled and finely diced

3 garlic cloves

2 red, yellow, or orange bell peppers, stemmed, deseeded, and cubed

2 pounds each collard greens, mustard greens, and kale, shredded

4 quarts water

1 cup apple cider vinegar

2 tablespoons Smokin' Hot 'n' Sweet Seasoning (page 77)

1 tablespoon pink Himalayan salt

IN A LARGE stockpot, heat the olive oil over medium-high heat. Add the onion and sauté until translucent, about 5 to 7 minutes. Add the garlic and caramelize, about 5 to 7 minutes more. Then add the peppers, stirring until they grow tender.

ADD 1 POUND of the greens, 2 quarts of the water, ½ cup of the vinegar, and 1 tablespoon of the seasoning. Cook down for 15 to 20 minutes, then add the remaining greens and the remaining water and vinegar. The liquids will also make a strong stock, full of nutrients pulled from those greens. Just before they are done, stir in the remaining tablespoon of seasoning and the salt. Serve immediately. Reserve the potlikker (nutrient-rich juices) for Potlikker Goobers (page 61).

Potlikker Goobers

We grew up calling peanuts "goobers." I was grown, though, before I learned that the word *goober* comes from the Gullah word *guba*, and is a derivative of *nguba*, the word for peanut in the Kimbundu language of western Angola. Peanuts are one of Georgia's chief crops, even today, and on the state's backroads and byways you'll find roadside stands and truck stops that sell boiled peanuts as a treat. When I was asked 15 years ago to make boiled peanuts for an event, I made them the way I grew up eating them—steeped in the salty goodness from the potlikker (nutrient-rich juices) of a Mess o' Greens (page 56).

SERVES 4

- 1½ cup sea salt, more if needed
- 1 gallon warm water
- 2 pounds unsalted raw peanuts in the shell
- 1 gallon potlikker, reserved from the Mess o' Greens (page 56)
- ¼ cup Berbere Spice Blend (page 77), more if needed

IN A LARGE stockpot, add 1 cup of the salt to the gallon of warm water and submerge the peanuts to soak overnight. You may have to use a plate to ensure the peanuts stay under the waterline, but they typically sink after they get waterlogged.

STRAIN OFF THE water and pour the potlikker over the peanuts. Add the berbere spices and the remaining ½ cup of sea salt and stir. Place the stockpot on the stovetop and set over high heat. Bring the peanuts to a rolling boil, then turn the heat to medium-low and slow boil for 30 minutes.

AFTER 30 MINUTES, turn the heat down to a simmer and allow to cook for 4 hours. (Keep an eye on the goobers and add water as needed.) At the 4-hour mark, pull out a few peanuts and check for softness and taste, ensuring that the peanuts are picking up the flavor from the berbere, salt, and potlikker. If the tastes are subdued beyond your liking, add another quarter cup each of salt and berbere spices and bring the peanuts back to a roaring boil, then turn down to a simmer.

COOK THE PEANUTS for another hour, checking the peanuts periodically for softness. If they are soft enough, remove the peanuts from the heat and let sit for 30 minutes to cool. Once they are at a handling temperature, spoon into bowls and start passing them around. Make sure you have extra bowls available for the discarded shells.

Curried Vegetable Galette

Vegetables were the stars on our tables, and they still are. Meat wasn't always readily available, but because farming families in the Brookman Community shared their harvests and we traded among ourselves, everyone had plenty to eat. We never knew hunger because of that collective spirit. I've always been drawn to rustic presentations, things made simply with caring hands, and a modest, unassuming galette represents that warmth and kindness to me. Serve alongside the Watermelon Steak Salad with Heirloom Tomatoes and Sangria Vinaigrette (page 65) for a balance of savory and sweet sensations.

SERVES 4 TO 6

FOR THE GALETTE DOUGH

2 cups all-purpose flour

½ cup finely ground white cornmeal

1 teaspoon Spike herb seasoning mix

½ teaspoon kosher salt

1 cup (2 sticks) cold unsalted butter, cubed

½ cup ice water

FOR THE CURRIED VEGETABLES

1 tablespoon olive oil

1 onion, julienned

1 small eggplant, julienned

1 purple potato, thinly sliced

1 teaspoon yellow curry powder

½ teaspoon pink Himalayan salt

2 tablespoons cashew butter

COMBINE THE FLOUR, cornmeal, herb seasoning, and salt in a medium bowl. Using two forks or a pastry blender, cut the butter into the flour mixture until it resembles coarse meal.

ADD ¼ CUP of the water and knead with your hands until the mixture turns into a dough. Add a tablespoon of water at a time until the dough is lightly tacky. Wrap the dough in plastic and place in the fridge until you are ready to assemble the galette.

IN A MEDIUM sauté pan over medium heat, heat the olive oil until fine wisps of smoke appear. Add the onion and eggplant, and sauté until the onions start to caramelize. Add the potatoes, curry, and salt and sauté for another minute. Remove the vegetables from the heat.

PLACE THE RACK in the middle of the oven and preheat the oven to 425°F. Line a baking sheet with parchment paper.

REMOVE THE DOUGH from the refrigerator and roll it out into a ½-inch-thick round on a lightly floured surface. Spread the dough with cashew butter, leaving a ½-inch border around the edges, then spoon the prepared vegetables over the butter.

FOLD THE EDGES of the dough over the vegetables to create a rustic crust. Place the galette on the prepared baking sheet and bake the galette for 15 to 20 minutes, until the crust is golden brown.

Watermelon Steak Salad with Heirloom Tomatoes and Sangria Vinaigrette

I grew up eating Georgia Rattlesnake watermelons—that's really what they're called, because the dark green stripes resemble a diamondback rattlesnake. These heirloom varietals, which can grow up to 40 pounds, have a deep reddish pink flesh that is sweeter than sweet. Folks started growing them around here in the 1830s. When I was a kid, we'd throw them in the back of the truck and take them to market. Because they are harder to come by now, and because people have grown accustomed to seedless watermelons, I created this recipe to accommodate either. But I absolutely prefer a rattlesnake watermelon, which we grow at Gilliard Farms.

SERVES 4 TO 6

FOR THE SALAD

1 to 1½ pounds freshly mixed salad greens or microgreens

1 pound heirloom tomatoes of varying sizes and colors, such as Cherokee Purple, Yellow Brandywine, black and yellow cherry tomatoes

¼ medium seedless watermelon (5 to 10 pounds)

Olive oil for brushing

FOR THE VINAIGRETTE

1 cup traditional red sangria, either homemade or store-bought

½ cup olive oil

Freshly cracked black pepper

Sea salt

PREPARE YOUR GRILL for medium-high direct heat, 375° to 450°F.

WHILE THE GRILL comes up to temperature, wash and dry the salad greens, then divide the greens among four to six serving plates. Wash and dry your tomatoes. Slice the whole tomatoes into ½-inch rounds and halve the cherry tomatoes. Divide and arrange the tomato slices evenly among the plates. Set the plates in the refrigerator to chill while you finish the dish.

SLICE THE WATERMELON into ¾-to-1-inch-thick "steaks," then quarter the steaks into wedges. Brush each side of the watermelon with a little olive oil, then set the wedges on the grill for approximately 3 minutes per side, until you get grill marks. The longer you leave the wedges on, the sweeter they'll get. Remove the watermelon from the grill and arrange evenly among the salad plates.

POUR THE SANGRIA into a large measuring cup with a pouring spout, then whisk the olive oil into the sangria until it makes a nice, loose vinaigrette. Generously dress the salads. Sprinkle the salads with pepper and salt to your liking, then serve.

Turn-Ups Two Ways

One day I noticed my fellow UC Santa Cruz students cutting off the tops of turnip greens and throwing them into the compost heap and feeding them to the chickens. That's when I introduced them to the sharp, peppery wonder of this versatile fall green that I grew up with. I knew about these greens because Nana never let us throw anything away. Using basically the same ingredients—turnips and mildly sweet cipollini onions—I showed them how to make two dishes. One is perfect during those unseasonably warm early days of October, when coastal Georgia summers refuse to give up the ghost. The other is an ideal side when the humidity dissipates, and you want something warm and comforting.

Turn-Up Salad

SERVES 4

4 to 6 tender turnips, bulbs peeled and thinly sliced, and greens roughly chopped

2 cipollini onions, minced

1 tablespoon apple cider vinegar

1 teaspoon fine sea salt

1 teaspoon freshly ground black pepper

6 tablespoons crème fraîche

Naan (page 48) for serving

IN A LARGE bowl, toss together the turnips, greens, onions, vinegar, salt, and pepper. Add the crème fraîche and toss some more, so that the greens are lightly coated.

SET THE BOWL in the refrigerator and chill for at least 1 hour. Serve plated on cold salad dishes with quarters of hot Naan.

Sautéed Turnips and Cipollini

SERVES 4

6 cipollini onions

2 tablespoons unsalted butter

1 teaspoon brown sugar

3 turnips, bulbs peeled and trimmed, greens julienned

¼ cup water

1 teaspoon fine sea salt

1 teaspoon coarsely ground black pepper

½ bunch basil, leaves cut in a chiffonade

PEEL AND TRIM the onions by immersing them in boiling water for 3 to 5 minutes. Remove them with a slotted spoon. Allow them to cool slightly, and then slip off the skin and cut in half.

MELT THE BUTTER in a large sauté pan over medium-low heat. Add the brown sugar and cook, stirring frequently, until the butter starts to brown, about 1 minute. Add the turnip bulbs and onions, swirling the pan to evenly coat. Add the water and cook until almost all the water has evaporated and the vegetables are glazed, about 20 minutes.

ADD THE TURNIP greens, cover, and continue cooking until the liquid has evaporated and the vegetables are caramelized, 3 to 5 minutes. Season with salt and pepper, adding more or less to taste. Transfer the turnips and onions to a large serving platter and garnish with fresh basil. This makes a great side dish for the Calypso Pork Loin (page 130).

TIP: *Want a third way to love turnips? Simply peel and dice the root, then roughly chop the greens, stems removed. You can reserve the stems for a future vegetable stock. Heat a drizzle of olive oil in a skillet over medium-high heat, then sauté the diced turnip for 5 to 7 minutes, until softened. Add the greens and sauté a minute or two more, until they wilt. Finish off with a dash of apple cider vinegar, salt, and pepper, then enjoy!*

Grandpa Arthur's Citrus-Candied Sweet Potatoes

As kids, my sister Althea and I spent our summers either in Bridgeport, Connecticut, with my dad's parents, who had traveled up from North Carolina during the Great Migration, or we headed south to Opa-locka, Florida, where my mother's father moved after her mother died. Whenever we rolled into the Moorish-style city of Opa-locka, Grandpa Arthur and Grandma Viola would have a big old pot of candied sweet potatoes and another pot full of rice ready and waiting—the Geechee comfort food!

SERVES 8 TO 12

- 1 cup cold salted butter (2 sticks), cut into pieces
- 4 pounds sweet potatoes, peeled and sliced into ¼-inch rounds
- 3½ cups freshly squeezed orange or satsuma juice
- 2 cups brown sugar
- ½ cup cornstarch, more if needed

IN A STOCKPOT large enough to hold the sweet potatoes, melt the butter over medium-high heat and stir until the butter starts to brown. Add the sweet potato rounds and coat with the brown butter. Cook for 5 minutes.

COMBINE 3 CUPS of the orange juice (reserving a half cup) with the brown sugar in a medium bowl and stir until the sugar starts to dissolve. Pour the mixture into the pot with the sweet potatoes and stir. Allow the liquid to come to a boil, and then turn the heat down to a simmer and let cook for 15 minutes.

TEST THE SWEET potatoes for doneness by piercing with a fork to see if they are tender. If they resist, they are not ready, and you will need to let them cook another 5 minutes. Repeat until they pass the fork-tender test.

MIX THE RESERVED ½ cup of orange juice with the cornstarch and stir until the mixture is combined and feels silky. (If mixture doesn't feel silky, add 1 tablespoon of cornstarch at a time until the mixture achieves the desired consistency.)

POUR HALF OF the cornstarch mixture into the candied yams and stir. Cook another minute, then add the remaining mixture. The sauce should thicken and coat the sweet potatoes.

Sweet Potatoes or Yams?

In the United States, we constantly confuse sweet potatoes and yams, even though they are two completely different root vegetables with different histories. Copper-colored or purple-fleshed sweet potatoes arrived in North America from South America. They are chock-full of beta-carotene. Yams, however, are essential to West African cooking traditions. Full of potassium, they have a starchy white, yellow, or rose-colored flesh and are covered in a brown, bark-like skin.

Slave traders carried yams in their ships, and even called the tubers by the West African word *nyam,* which means "eat." But when my ancestors arrived on these shores, sweet potatoes were the closest thing they had to the cornerstone of their cooking, and they became the substitute for the yam.

If you can find a true yam, try substituting it for any of these recipes that call for sweet potatoes. You will discover a much subtler flavor and a more robust texture that is more authentic to African foodways.

Sweet Potato Pone

This sweet-spicy concoction is a tasty take on corn pone, but its consistency is more similar to a corn pudding—fluffy but textured, not only from the pecan (pronounced PEE-can in these parts) crust, but also from the grated sweet potatoes folded into the mix. This recipe calls for molasses, but sorghum syrup or pure cane syrup—like the kind my elders used to press from purple ribbon cane—are lush cup-to-cup substitutes. When I have it on hand, I use Almost Rum, a cane syrup produced by the local single-estate distiller, Richland Rum.

SERVES 12

1 cup brown sugar

½ cup (1 stick) unsalted butter, softened, plus 2 tablespoons reserved

4 eggs

1 cup molasses or pure cane syrup

One 12-ounce can evaporated milk

1 teaspoon pure vanilla extract

1 teaspoon lemon extract

1 teaspoon ground cinnamon

1 teaspoon ground nutmeg

⅛ teaspoon ground allspice

⅛ teaspoon ground cloves

½ teaspoon kosher salt

4 large sweet potatoes, peeled and grated

4 large sweet potatoes, roasted, peeled, and mashed

2 cups chopped pecans

IN THE BOWL of a stand mixer using the paddle attachment, cream together the brown sugar and butter on high speed until light and fluffy, approximately 3 minutes. Add the eggs one at a time until incorporated, then add the molasses, milk, extracts, and spices until just incorporated.

PREHEAT THE OVEN to 350°F. With the reserved 2 tablespoons of butter, grease twelve 4-ounce ramekins. Set the ramekins on a baking sheet.

REMOVE THE BOWL from the mixer and fold the grated and mashed sweet potatoes into the sugar-spice mixture. Fill each ramekin about three-quarters full with the sweet potato pone mixture. Place the ramekins in the oven and bake for 20 minutes.

REMOVE THE RAMEKINS from the oven and sprinkle the pone with a healthy layer of chopped pecans. Place the sheet of ramekins back in the oven and bake for another 15 minutes. Use a toothpick to check for doneness. Once the pone is done and you've pulled the ramekins out of the oven, let rest for 5 minutes, then serve and enjoy.

Sweet Potato and Red Pepper Soup

Have you ever wanted to make something super yummy and didn't have the ingredients on hand? This soup is a result of one such happy accident. I had a hankering for butternut squash soup, but all I had in the pantry were some sweet potatoes and a red pepper. Now, this is my go-to soup. It pairs beautifully with grilled cheese, seasoned croutons, or a crusty hunk of bread.

SERVES 4 TO 6

1 large red pepper, seeded and diced

4 garlic cloves, peeled and roughly chopped

2 pounds sweet potatoes, peeled, medium diced

¼ cup Vidalia onion, small diced

1 teaspoon Frontier Co-op Applewood Smoked Sea Salt

1 teaspoon olive oil

1 teaspoon cayenne

1 quart Vegetable Stock (page 34)

PREHEAT THE OVEN to 375°F and line a baking sheet with parchment paper.

IN A LARGE bowl, toss the pepper, garlic, sweet potatoes, onion, salt, olive oil, and cayenne until well coated. Place the vegetables in a single layer on the prepared baking sheet and place the pan in the oven for 15 to 20 minutes, until the pepper and onions start to char.

POUR THE STOCK into a heavy-bottomed stockpot and bring it to a simmer over medium heat. Add the roasted vegetables and let simmer for 20 minutes more.

USING AN UPRIGHT blender, pour half of the soup into the carafe, place the lid on top without the blender lid cap, and using a towel as cover, pulse the blender until the vegetables are pureed and smooth. Pour the soup into bowls and repeat with the other half of the soup. Enjoy. Store leftovers (if there are any) in the refrigerator up to 1 week.

Giardiniera

My Nana never let a bumper crop of seasonal vegetables go to waste. Twice a year, she would kick out her husband, Mr. Killens, and his cigars from his game room and cover the pool table with a large sheet of plywood. That would become the all-hands-on-deck canning table. We would each be given a task, from cutting up vegetables to distilling muscadine wine through clean white pillowcases. This giardiniera recipe is an homage to Nana's pickled vegetables, which we ate straight out of the jar, as a side to barbecue, or on a relish dish with deviled eggs. That old game room is now my teaching and testing kitchen, and our shelves are filled with dried herbs and spices, preserves, and Jovan's kombucha.

MAKES 4 TO 6 PINTS

FOR THE MARINADE

2 cups apple cider vinegar

1 cup olive oil

1 teaspoon fennel seeds

1 teaspoon celery seed

½ teaspoon sugar

½ teaspoon sea salt

4 to 6 bay leaves

FOR THE GIARDINIERA

1 red onion, thinly sliced

1 lemon, thinly sliced and seeded

1 head cauliflower, each crown cut in half

2 large carrots, washed and thinly sliced on the diagonal

2 stalks celery, thinly sliced

1 red bell pepper, seeded and thinly sliced

1 orange bell pepper, seeded and thinly sliced

1 Scotch bonnet pepper

3 cups apple cider vinegar

3 cups water

2 tablespoons sea salt

1 tablespoon granulated sugar

2 juniper berries

1 sprig oregano

1 teaspoon fennel seeds

¼ teaspoon black peppercorns

FOLLOW MANUFACTURER'S INSTRUCTIONS for sterilizing four to six 16-ounce mason jars.

IN A LARGE nonreactive bowl, whisk together all the marinade ingredients except the bay leaves and set aside.

(CONTINUED)

PLACE ALL THE vegetables and Scotch bonnet in a large stock-pot and cover with the vinegar, water, salt, sugar, juniper berries, oregano, fennel seeds, and peppercorns. Over medium heat, bring to a low boil for 5 minutes, then remove from the heat and let stand for 30 minutes.

STRAIN THE VEGETABLES, reserving 1 cup of the liquid. Distribute vegetables evenly among the mason jars.

COMBINE THE 1 CUP RESERVED liquid with the marinade and pour the liquid over the vegetables. Add one bay leaf to each jar, then seal, cover, and refrigerate for at least 24 hours. Serve the giardiniera chilled. The vegetables will keep for 14 days in the refrigerator.

VARIATION

For a sweet-sour variation using fruit, eliminate the Scotch bonnet pepper and substitute the following:

8 large peaches, pitted and sliced, for the cauliflower
4 plums, pitted and quartered, for the carrots
2 Granny Smith apples, cored and medium diced, for the celery

FOLLOW ALL THE instructions for making the giardiniera. Serve chilled as a condiment for roasted meats, on a cheese platter, or as a complement to pound cake or cheesecake.

CheFarmer's Gazpacho

When I returned to Glynn County, Georgia, after vowing never to come back, my life somewhat paralleled those of my great uncles, who worked at the Jekyll Island Club during the week and farmed over the weekends. I served as the executive chef for the Lodge on Little St. Simons Island, an all-inclusive eco-resort accessible only by boat. There, I got reacquainted with the land and waterways I had taken for granted as a child, and I began to see them with new eyes and listened to the voices of those elders. This gazpacho recipe came out of my wanting to share the bounty of this land with our guests.

SERVES 6 TO 8

- 4 cups tomato juice
- 8 Cherokee Purple tomatoes, chopped and seeded
- 2 lemon cucumbers, chopped
- 1 medium red onion, chopped
- 1 medium Vidalia onion, chopped
- 1 red bell pepper, chopped and seeded
- 3 tablespoons kosher salt
- 2 tablespoons cumin
- 1 elephant garlic clove, peeled and roughly chopped
- ½ teaspoon cayenne pepper
- ¾ cup red wine vinegar
- Crème fraîche for serving

ADD THE INGREDIENTS in stages into the bowl of a food processor—first the tomato juice and tomatoes, then the cucumbers and onions, then the bell pepper, then the salt, cumin, garlic, and cayenne pepper, finishing with the vinegar—and pulse until you achieve the desired consistency (not pure liquid, but thoroughly combined and textured). Taste and adjust seasonings accordingly. Serve chilled with a dollop of crème fraîche.

Chow Chow

Another essential condiment my Nana made represents the Southern response to sauerkraut. Chow Chow has Acadian origins out of Louisiana, and its name comes from the French word for cabbage, or *chou*. This piquant accompaniment finishes with a brief dazzle of heat, and it is excellent alongside the Smoked Ossabaw Island Hog (page 119) or the Farmhouse Burger with Tomato Jam (page 146).

MAKES 6 JARS

6 medium Vidalia onions, peeled and roughly diced

2 medium green bell peppers, seeded and diced

2 medium red bell peppers, seeded and diced

2 medium firm green tomatoes, seeded and diced

1 small green cabbage, cored and sliced

1 tablespoon kosher salt

½ cup water

½ cup apple cider vinegar

¾ cup brown sugar

1 teaspoon celery seed

1½ teaspoons mustard seed

¾ teaspoon dry mustard

½ teaspoon ground turmeric

¼ teaspoon red pepper flakes

¼ teaspoon ground ginger

STERILIZE SIX 16-OUNCE mason jars according to manufacturer's instructions.

IN A LARGE colander, toss the onions, peppers, tomatoes, and cabbage with the salt and let sit for 15 minutes.

WHILE THE VEGETABLES settle, combine the water, vinegar, sugar, seeds, and remaining spices together in a large nonreactive pot. Over high heat, bring the pickling juice to a rolling boil for 5 minutes, ensuring that the sugar is fully dissolved. Remove the liquid from the heat and allow it to cool to room temperature.

DIVIDE THE VEGETABLE medley among the canning jars and pour the pickling juices evenly over the vegetables. Seal and store in the refrigerator until ready to use. The Chow Chow will keep for 4 weeks.

Spices and Seasonings

Now, more than ever, you can find spices and seasonings from around the world in the grocery store. Even still, I like to make my own spice-and-seasoning blends so that I can modulate the heat and enhance the layers. With a simple coffee or spice grinder, you can do the same.

Smokin' Hot 'n' Sweet Seasoning

MAKES ½ CUP

¼ cup smoked paprika

¼ cup steak seasoning

1 teaspoon cayenne pepper

MIX THE INGREDIENTS. Store in an airtight container in a cool, dry place for up to 6 weeks.

Berbere Spice Blend

MAKES 3 CUPS

¼ cup whole black peppercorns

¼ cup cumin seeds

10 whole cloves

2 tablespoons cardamom seeds

2 tablespoons fenugreek seeds

½ cup smoked paprika

¼ cup cayenne pepper

¼ cup garlic powder

¼ cup onion powder

¼ cup finely ground Sumatra coffee

2 tablespoons ground coriander

2 tablespoons pink Himalayan salt

2 tablespoons ground turmeric

2 tablespoons ground ginger

1 tablespoon ground cinnamon

IN A NONSTICK skillet over medium heat, toast the peppercorns, cumin seeds, cloves, and cardamom and fenugreek seeds for 2 minutes. Remove the spices from the heat and allow them to cool to room temperature.

COMBINE ALL THE remaining seasonings in an airtight container and mix well. Once the toasted spices have cooled, finely grind the toasted spices in small batches in a coffee or spice grinder, then add them to the container. Store in a cool, dry place for up to 2 months.

TIP: *The deep umber of this fragrant Ethiopian staple only hints at the bright burst of heat that follows. In addition to soups and stews, berbere spices are a flavorful rub for short ribs and lamb.*

De Wata / Water

The Gullah Geechee are defined by their relationship to water. It is where we go to feed our families. It is where we return time and again to seek guidance from the ancestors. My family are descended from the Freshwater Geechee, the ones who reshaped the land to craft irrigation systems for rice fields from the brackish rivers and creeks. The Saltwater Geechee farmed cotton and indigo on the Sea Islands and later steered the flat-bottomed bateaux to harvest oysters, which was one of the region's strongest industries until its collapse in the middle of the last century. Even as a mainlander, I have always had one foot in the soil and one in the ocean.

When my mom cleaned houses on St. Simons Island, I learned from the old timers at the pier how to fish. I had a little string tied to my finger, with bait on the end. I would just drop the string in the water and feel the fish playing with the bait. I eventually caught enough fish to sell so that I could buy my own fishing pole. I met a man there who taught me how to make my own crab net. Because of rising and warming seas, loss of ancestral lands to developers, and my own generation's leaving to find jobs in cities, this way of life—the self-sufficiency to never know hunger—is disappearing.

When I was a little older, when my dad went to work at the port docks in Brunswick, he would leave me at Overlook Park to fish for mullet. I used the "snatch" method of throwing out a handful of chicken mash to call forth those gray, oily fish; then I'd toss in a three-pronged hook to snatch as many as I could.

I think that's why I'm so drawn to a tradition we have here called the Blessing of the Fleet. Every Mother's Day in Brunswick, the old Portuguese ritual of asking for the safe passage and prosperous haul of the fishing and shrimping fleets takes place. Shrimpers festoon their trawlers in brilliant flags and parade down the Brunswick River to the ocean, where the priest from St. Francis Xavier drops a flower anchor into the sea to honor the souls of departed fishermen.

The Gullah Geechee people say that "de wata bring we and de wata gwine tek we bak." It's a reminder that how we treat our waters reflects how we treat each other.

Fried Mullet and Roe

In some parts of the United States, mullet is considered a trash or bait fish, but it is sustenance to us along the Georgia coast. And there were many times I'd snatch enough of them to feed our whole family. We'd clean the fish and fry them, including the roe—a kind of poor man's caviar—and serve it with rice or grits. Imagine my surprise when I attended the international Slow Food conference, Terra Madre, in Italy, and saw that bottarga, a fried mullet roe, was considered a fine-dining delicacy. You can serve the mullet on white bread shellacked with hot mustard, just like we'd get them on Fridays at the local churches, or you can serve over CheFarmer's Grits (page 29) with fried mullet roe when it's available, usually during the fall.

SERVES 4

4 mullet fillets

1 teaspoon sea salt

1 cup buttermilk, store-bought or homemade

1 teaspoon freshly ground black pepper

1 teaspoon dried Italian seasoning

2 teaspoons curry powder

1 cup all-purpose flour

1 cup vegetable oil

Fried Mullet Roe (recipe follows)

Rice Grits (page 141) or CheFarmer's Grits (page 29) for serving (optional)

IN A LARGE bowl, season the mullet with the salt and pour the buttermilk over the fillets. Set the bowl aside until ready to fry.

IN A SHALLOW bowl, combine the pepper, Italian seasoning, curry powder, and flour.

IN A DEEP cast-iron skillet, heat the vegetable oil on high heat until it reaches 350° to 375°F, according to a deep-fry or candy thermometer.

PULL EACH MULLET fillet out of the buttermilk and dredge through the flour mixture, and then place each fillet in the hot oil. When the fillets have turned a dark golden brown all over, remove from the oil and drain on paper towels. Serve while warm with Fried Mullet Roe, and with Rice Grits or CheFarmer's Grits, if desired.

Fried Mullet Roe (or Bottarga)

SERVES 4

2 mullet roe

1 cup milk

2 tablespoons plus
  2 teaspoons olive oil

1 large yellow onion,
  julienned

2 teaspoons fine sea salt

1 teaspoon cracked black
  pepper

1 teaspoon granulated garlic

1 teaspoon chili powder

1 cup flour

½ cup cornmeal

RINSE THE ROE and slice into ¼-inch pieces, then place in a bowl with the milk.

HEAT 2 TEASPOONS of the olive oil in a skillet on high, then add the onions and 1 teaspoon of the salt. Toss the onions occasionally, until they soften and slightly caramelize to a light brown, approximately 10 to 12 minutes.

IN A SEPARATE bowl, combine the remaining salt, pepper, garlic, chili powder, flour, and cornmeal.

ONCE THE ONIONS have reached the desired softness and sweetness, add the remaining 2 tablespoons oil to the skillet and turn down to a medium-high heat. Push the onions to one side of the skillet to continue caramelizing. Remove the roe from the milk and dredge through the flour mixture and place in the hot pan, searing and cooking each side for 4 minutes. Serve the roe hot with the onions, with or without fried mullet fillets.

Fried Fish and Grits

My great-grandfather Horace used to go fishing early nearly every morning. He'd catch a mess. Sometimes he brought back whiting, other times croaker, butterfish, or drum. He'd start a stew of tomatoes, onions, and fresh okra pulled fresh from the field, then dredge the fish in cornmeal and panfry it in a skillet. This was our breakfast, our bacon and eggs.

SERVES 4

FOR THE FISH

4 fish fillets

1 teaspoon sea salt

1 cup buttermilk, store-bought or homemade

1 teaspoon freshly ground black pepper

1 cup cornmeal or all-purpose flour, based on your preference

1 cup vegetable oil

CheFarmer's Grits (page 29)

FOR THE STEWED OKRA

3 tablespoons unsalted butter

1 onion, finely diced

1 pint okra, sliced

4 large beefsteak tomatoes, roughly chopped

2 teaspoons sea salt

½ teaspoon cracked black pepper

IN A LARGE bowl, season the fish fillets with the salt and pour the buttermilk over the fillets. Set the bowl aside until ready to fry.

IN A SHALLOW bowl, combine the pepper and cornmeal or flour.

IN A DEEP cast-iron skillet, heat the vegetable oil on high heat until it reaches 350° to 375°F, according to a deep-fry or candy thermometer.

PULL EACH FILLET out of the buttermilk and dredge through the cornmeal or flour mixture, and then place each fillet in the hot oil. When the fillets have turned a dark golden brown all over, remove from the oil and drain on paper towels.

IN ANOTHER SKILLET, melt the butter over medium heat. Once it turns brown, add the onions and the okra and sauté for 2 minutes. Add the tomatoes, salt, and pepper and continue cooking, stirring frequently, until the skin on the tomatoes begins to blister. Remove the stewed okra from the heat.

TO SERVE, SPOON a healthy dose of grits on a plate. Set a fillet on the grits, then spoon the okra and tomatoes over the fish and grits. You'll be ready to face the day after a plate.

Grandma Florine's Salmon Cakes on Pepper Rice

When the fish weren't biting, my great-grandmother Florine would have canned salmon on hand. She'd mix it with bread crumbs and finely diced onions and peppers to make these little croquettes. My Nana and my mom did likewise. They would serve them with a healthy side of tartar sauce for an inexpensive seafood dinner. Later on, when I made staff meals, I would save the sweet-savory meat from the tail pieces of salmon and make these hearty cakes that were inspired by my family's recipe, and I'd serve them with chili-powder-infused rice. Full of protein and carbs, they helped us power through the night's service.

MAKES 12 CAKES

¼ cup vegetable oil

Two 14-ounce cans salmon, picked of bones and skin, or 1 pound fresh salmon, skin removed

1 teaspoon sea salt, if using fresh salmon

1 teaspoon freshly ground black pepper

1 large egg, beaten

1 tablespoon all-purpose flour

2 scallions, white and green parts roughly chopped

HEAT THE OIL in a deep cast-iron skillet or pan on high heat until it reaches 375°F.

IF USING FRESH salmon, grind it and the salt in a food processor until it is a fine, flaky meat.

IN A BOWL, combine the salmon, pepper, egg, flour, and scallions. With a small ice cream scoop or tablespoon, take 4 ounces of the salmon mixture and shape it into a cake. Repeat until all cakes are made.

PLACE THE CAKES into the oil and cook until golden brown on each side. For canned salmon, approximately 2 minutes per side; for fresh salmon, 4 minutes per side. Drain the cakes on paper towels, then serve on a bed of pepper rice.

(CONTINUED)

Pepper Rice

SERVES 4 TO 6

2 cups water

1 teaspoon fine sea salt

1 cup Anson Mills Carolina
   Gold Rice, Congaree and
   Penn Jupiter Brown Rice,
   or another long-grain rice

½ to 1 teaspoon ground
   cayenne pepper,
   depending on how spicy
   you like it

½ to 1 teaspoon cracked
   black pepper, depending
   on how spicy you like it

IN A MEDIUM saucepan with a lid, add the water and salt, then bring to a rolling boil over high heat. Add the rice and peppers, turn the heat down to a simmer, cover, and cook the rice without stirring. Once the water is fully absorbed and the rice is tender, approximately 18 to 20 minutes, remove from the heat and fluff with a fork.

Gullah Fish Stew

The gift of Gullah Geechee cooking is learning how to stretch and feed a lot of people with a little bit of this and that, stewed in tomatoes, and well-seasoned. That's why you'll find several one-pot recipes throughout this book. We used whatever fish we caught—whiting, sheepshead, or bream—and tossed in some shrimp and leftover crabmeat. What I learned when I was traveling with the military is that what we were making in coastal Georgia wasn't all that different—except for the spices and types of seafood—than a chreime in North Africa or a cioppino in Southern Italy.

SERVES 12

4 tablespoons olive oil

1 large yellow onion, finely diced

4 garlic cloves, minced

10 new potatoes, diced

1 tablespoon sea salt

1 teaspoon salt-free vegetable-pepper seasoning blend

½ teaspoon cayenne pepper

3 pounds medium fresh tomatoes, diced and seeded (or one 35-ounce can diced tomatoes)

2 quarts (8 cups) Fish Stock (recipe follows) or store-bought

1 bag Sapelo Sea Farms clams, 40 to 50 count

1½ pounds sheepshead or other firm, meaty fish, cut into 2-inch chunks

Crusty bread for serving

HEAT THE OIL in a large pot on medium heat, then add the onions, garlic, and potatoes. Sauté along with the salt, vegetable pepper, and cayenne until the onions soften and start to turn brown, approximately 7 to 10 minutes. Add the tomatoes and fish stock and bring to a boil.

ADD THE CLAMS and let cook for 3 minutes, then turn the heat down low to simmer. Add the fish chunks and continue cooking the stew until the fish becomes firm but flaky, approximately 3 to 5 minutes.

SERVE HOT WITH a side of crusty bread for dipping in the broth.

TIP: *If you want a stew with thicker consistency, incorporate 1 to 2 tablespoons of an arrowroot slurry.*

Did You Know?

Sheepshead and porgy, or bream, are carnivores. These fish feed on shellfish, such as shrimp, small crabs, and prawns. This diet imparts a sweet, rich flavor and tender texture to the fish.

Fish Stock

MAKES 8 CUPS

FOR THE HERB SACHET
Cheesecloth
4 whole peppercorns
4 sprigs thyme
2 bay leaves
2 whole cloves
½ bunch parsley

FOR THE STOCK
1 tablespoon butter
1 tablespoon olive oil
2 ribs celery, roughly chopped
1 large onion, peeled and roughly chopped
1 carrot, roughly chopped
3 pounds white fish bones (if using heads, make sure the gills have been removed)
1 gallon water

LAY A DOUBLED piece of cheesecloth flat on the countertop. Place all the sachet aromatics in the center of the cloth, then gather the corners together to make a pouch. Tie the corners together or use kitchen twine or string to do so. Leave one length of the twine long enough to tie to the stockpot handles so that you can remove it easily. Set the sachet aside.

IN A LARGE stockpot on medium heat, melt the butter and warm the olive oil. Add the celery, onion, and carrot, and sauté until the onion is translucent, 3 to 5 minutes. Add the fish bones and water and bring to a low simmer. Add the sachet.

LET THE STOCK cook for one hour, periodically skimming the top for impurities. Once the stock has cooked, let it cool to room temperature, then strain it through a fine mesh sieve into airtight pint or quart containers to freeze for up to 6 months or refrigerate up to 4 days.

Snapper on the Half Shell

A friend who used to dine frequently at The Farmer & The Larder, my former restaurant in Brunswick, was one of those guys who thought mullet was trash food and swore he would never eat it . . . until I served it to him at the restaurant and changed his mind forever. Then he suggested I make Snapper on the Half Shell, a dish he had grown up with on the Gulf. Red snapper remains one of my all-time favorite summer catches. It is such a beautiful presentation, served whole (page 92) or stuffed, and the mild but firm white flesh has an almost roasted pecan-like flavor. I had never prepared and served it halved lengthwise with the scales still intact to create a stable shell for lifting out the tender flaky meat, but it's forever part of my repertoire now.

SERVES 4

2 red snapper fillets with skins and scales intact

2 pinches of sea salt

4 tablespoons unsalted butter, room temperature

½ teaspoon cracked black pepper

1 teaspoon smoked paprika

2 garlic cloves, peeled and smashed

1 bunch cilantro or flat-leaf parsley, roughly chopped

Juice of 1 lime

2 tablespoons coconut oil

PREHEAT THE OVEN to 400°F.

WASH EACH SNAPPER fillet with cold water and pat dry. Sprinkle each fillet all over with the sea salt, then set aside.

IN A BOWL, mix together the butter, pepper, paprika, garlic, cilantro, and lime to create an easily spreadable, herbed butter.

IN A LARGE cast-iron skillet, melt the coconut oil over medium heat. Turn the heat to medium-high, then add the snapper fillets, skin side down. Using a pastry brush, slather each fillet evenly with half the herbed butter. Once the skin has slightly charred, approximately 3 minutes, slide the skillet into the oven and cook the fish until it is flaky, approximately 15 minutes. Baste the fish every 5 minutes or so with the remaining herbed butter.

ONCE THE FISH is done, remove the skillet from the oven and plate the fish—skin, shell, and all—using a long, narrow, slotted spatula.

NOTE: *If you are cooking on a grill, be sure to rub the fillet skin and the grill grates with coconut oil. Once the grill temperature reaches 400°F, grill the fillets, covered with the skin side down.*

Whole Red Stripe Snapper

For a completely different but no less dramatic presentation of snapper, I turn to Jamaica, which is known not only for its spicy-hot jerk seasoning but also for its Red Stripe beer—an English-style lager with caramel undernotes that burnishes the fish with an amber glow.

SERVES 2 TO 4

1 large whole red snapper, cleaned with skin on but no scales

1 teaspoon sea salt

1 teaspoon freshly ground black pepper

2 teaspoons Jerk Seasoning (recipe follows)

½ bunch parsley

1 lime, quartered

2 Scotch bonnet peppers, split and seeds removed

One 24-ounce bottle Red Stripe beer

PREPARE YOUR GRILL for indirect cooking on low heat, bringing the grill to between 225°F and 240°F.

LAY OUT A sheet of aluminum foil to hold and wrap the whole fish. Place the fish in the middle of the foil, then cut three diagonal slits on each side of the fish. Sprinkle the fish all over with salt and pepper, then rub the insides of the fish with the jerk seasoning. Fill the cavity with the parsley, lime, and peppers. Fold up the sides of the foil so that it creates an open packet, then pour about half of the Red Stripe over the fish. It is necessary to provide moisture for fish when grilling, or the fish will dry out quickly.

FOLD THE EDGES of the foil over one another to completely seal the packet like a loose tent, not touching the fish and so that no steam can escape.

PLACE THE FISH packet on the hot grill and cover. After 10 minutes, open the grill carefully and unroll the packet just enough to pour the remaining half of the Red Stripe over the fish. Close the fish packet by rolling the foil back down.

CLOSE THE GRILL and let cook for another 10 minutes. Check the fish for doneness by unrolling the packet and seeing if the fish flakes easily with a fork. If not, let the fish cook for another 5 minutes, then check again.

ONCE DONE, REMOVE the fish packet from the grill and place on a large platter. Carefully unroll the packet. The steam and smell should have you salivating at this point. Slide the foil from under the fish so that you have a whole fish presentation for the table.

(CONTINUED)

TO SERVE, USE a serving spoon and fork to remove the pin bones from the top and bottom of the fish. Then, using the serving fork or knife, peel back the skin and remove the top fillets and plate them. This will expose the spine and feathery rib cage and head, which you can remove by pulling up from the tail. (There is meat in the cheeks, so be sure to remove those and serve them as well.) Remove any remaining fine bones on the bottom fillets, then plate the bottom two fillets. Drizzle them with a little olive oil and enjoy.

TIP: *To choose the freshest fish from the fishmonger, if you don't happen to catch it yourself, make sure the eyes are bulging and clear, the skin glistens, and the scales are tight (not dry and flaking off). It should smell briny, like the sea, not sharp, like ammonia, or even "fishy."*

Jerk Seasoning

MAKES 1 CUP

2 tablespoons garlic powder

2 tablespoons onion powder

1 tablespoon cayenne pepper

1 tablespoon smoked paprika

1 tablespoon crushed red pepper flakes

2 teaspoons dried thyme

2 teaspoons dried parsley

1 teaspoon ground allspice

1 teaspoon ground cumin

1 teaspoon ground nutmeg

1 teaspoon ground cloves

1 teaspoon ground cinnamon

MIX ALL THE ingredients together in a pint-sized mason jar, cover, and shake until all the spices are well incorporated. Store in a cool, dry place for up to 6 months.

Smokin' Hot 'n' Sweet Crab Dip

Even though my dad was a masterful baker, he was unable to get a job as a pastry chef or cook when we moved back to Brunswick in the early 1970s. So he took a job as a crab boiler at the Lewis Crab Factory. The boats would come in and he would work in the chill of winter or the heat of summer all night boiling those crabs so they would be ready for the pickers the next morning. I developed this recipe as an ode to him.

SERVES 4 TO 6

2 pounds fresh or canned lump crabmeat

2 tablespoons Smokin' Hot 'n' Sweet Seasoning (page 77)

1 tablespoon Frontier Co-op Applewood-smoked Sea Salt

1 teaspoon ground sumac

1 quart (4 cups) heavy cream

2 tablespoons holy trinity blend (equal parts onions, celery, green pepper)

8 ounces cream cheese, softened and room temperature

8 ounces goat cheese or no-rind brie, softened and room temperature

Garlic Beer Bread (page 42) for serving

TOSS THE CRABMEAT with the Smokin' Hot 'n' Sweet Seasoning, salt, and sumac and set aside.

PLACE THE HEAVY cream in a heavy-bottomed saucepan with the holy trinity and warm over medium heat for 5 minutes. Add the cheeses and stir until they have melted and the mixture has thickened. Gently stir in the crabmeat until well incorporated, then remove from the heat.

TRANSFER THE CRAB dip to a bowl and serve with Garlic Beer Bread.

Crab Diablo

"Devil crab" is a signature Gullah Geechee dish. It is served by packing seasoned crabmeat back into the shell and baking until the mixture turns golden brown. Every family recipe is a little different and a closely guarded secret. When I was 17 years old, I drove my little car to the juke joints around Brunswick and sold my girlfriend's grandmother's devil crabs, wrapped up in foil, for one or two dollars each. The proprietors expected them. "Are these from Grandma Pinkney?" they'd ask, and when I'd say, "Yes," they'd ask for a dozen or more. I learned from her to smell the crabmeat first. "Crab will tell you what it needs," Grandma Pinkney would say. And to this day, mine always answers: lots of lump meat, a little egg white, scallions, and cayenne pepper.

MAKES 12

12 blue crab shells for stuffing

2 pounds crabmeat

2 egg whites, whipped until frothy

2 scallions, finely sliced

1 red pepper, finely diced

2 teaspoons cayenne pepper

2 teaspoons sea salt

1 teaspoon smoked paprika

PREHEAT THE OVEN to 400°F and line a baking sheet with parchment paper or foil. Wash and pat dry the crab shells and set aside.

IN A LARGE bowl, combine the crabmeat, egg whites, scallions, red pepper, cayenne, salt, and paprika. (If the crabmeat smells like the salt of the sea, you can use less salt if you would like.) Gently toss all the ingredients until well combined.

STUFF EACH CRAB shell evenly with the crab mixture, as if you were making a crab cake. Place the shells on the prepared baking sheet and bake for 10 minutes.

PULL THE BAKING sheet out of the oven and, using a thermometer, test to see if the internal temperature has hit 165°F. If so, the crabs are ready to remove from the oven. If not, place them back in oven in 3-minute intervals until the temperature reaches 165°F. Serve warm or wrap each shell in foil for a later date. The Crab Diablo will keep for 5 days in the refrigerator. Reheat in the foil at 350°F for 15 minutes.

Effie's Shrimp Creole

When folks think of coastal Georgia food, they think of shrimp and grits. That dish is definitely indicative of the Saltwater Gullah and Geechee who lived on the Sea Islands. They most often made the dish with a rich brown gravy or roux, much more akin to a gumbo. Freshwater—or mainland—Geechee, like my family, made something closer to a jambalaya, no okra but richly flavored with tomatoes and red pepper. The rice, of course, stretches it. For me, my mom's shrimp creole, a recipe handed down through the family, is a comfort food.

SERVES 4

2 tablespoons unsalted butter

1 yellow onion, finely diced

3 garlic cloves, peeled and minced

1 green bell pepper, seeded and finely diced

1 red bell pepper, seeded and finely diced

1 orange bell pepper, seeded and finely diced

One 16-ounce can tomato puree

1 tablespoon red pepper flakes

2 cups uncooked long-grain rice or Carolina Gold Rice

1 quart warm Shrimp Stock, prepared or homemade (recipe follows)

2 pounds large shrimp, peeled and deveined, shells reserved for Shrimp Stock

Fine sea salt and freshly ground black pepper

IN A LARGE cast-iron skillet, melt the butter over medium heat. Stir in the onions and garlic, and sauté until golden brown, about 5 minutes.

ADD THE PEPPERS, tomato puree, red pepper flakes, and rice, stirring until well combined. Pour the stock in slowly to prevent splattering, as the pan will be hot, then bring the creole to a boil. Once boiling, stir, cover, then reduce the heat to low and simmer for 15 minutes.

REMOVE THE COVER, add the shrimp, and give the rice a good stir. Cook for 5 to 7 minutes more, until all the liquid is absorbed and the shrimp have pinked and curled. Before serving, taste and add salt and pepper to your liking. Serve and enjoy.

(CONTINUED)

Shrimp Stock

MAKES 2 QUARTS

2 quarts (8 cups) cold water

4 cups shrimp shells

1 tablespoon olive oil

1 Vidalia onion, peeled and quartered

1 carrot, roughly chopped

1 celery rib, cut into 2-inch pieces, including leaves

1 lemon, quartered

2 bay leaves

2 sprigs thyme

1 tablespoon kosher salt

1 teaspoon whole black peppercorns

POUR THE WATER in a large stockpot and set aside.

RINSE AND DRAIN the shrimp shells. In a large skillet, heat the oil over medium-high heat and toss the shrimp shells for 2 minutes. Add the onions, carrots, and celery and cook, stirring, for 2 to 3 minutes more.

ADD THE SHRIMP shells and vegetables to the stockpot, then toss in the lemon, bay leaves, thyme, salt, and pepper. Bring the stock to a boil, then reduce heat and simmer for 40 minutes. Remove from the heat, then strain the stock through a cheesecloth-lined sieve into quart- or pint-sized containers. Cool the stock completely, then refrigerate for up to 2 weeks or freeze for later use.

Coastal Paella

When people think paella, the slow-cooking, seafood-infused rice dish, they think Spain, Cuba, and the Caribbean. I would argue, however, that it has all the attributes of the Georgia coast—one-pot cookery, Spanish influences, long-grain rice, the bounty of the ocean. We may have used turmeric because we didn't have access to saffron threads, but the seafood and rice dishes we made, they had ties to other places. No matter where I've been, whether Georgia, Florida, or Spain, paella always reminds me of home. It's worth the wait, and as my Nana would always say, "You can't rush the goodness, baby!"

SERVES 6 TO 8

- 4 tablespoons olive oil
- 3 cups long-grain rice
- 3 cloves garlic, peeled and minced
- 1 teaspoon crushed red pepper flakes
- 1 pinch saffron threads
- 1 bay leaf
- ½ bunch flat-leaf parsley, chopped
- 1 quart seafood stock
- 2 lemons, zested and quartered
- 1 yellow onion, chopped
- 1 red bell pepper, medium diced
- 1 pound smoked sausage, thinly sliced
- 30 Sapelo Sea Farms clams
- 1½ pounds large Wild Georgia shrimp, peeled and deveined

HEAT 2 TABLESPOONS of the olive oil in a large skillet or paella pan over medium heat. Stir in the rice, garlic, and red pepper flakes. Cook, stirring to coat rice with oil, about 3 minutes. Stir in the saffron threads, bay leaf, parsley, seafood stock, and lemon zest. Bring to a boil, cover, and reduce heat to medium-low. Simmer 20 minutes without stirring.

MEANWHILE, HEAT THE remaining 2 tablespoons olive oil in a separate skillet over medium heat. Stir in the onion and cook for 5 minutes. Add the bell pepper and sausage and cook 5 more minutes.

AFTER THE RICE has cooked for 20 minutes, remove the cover on the rice and transfer the sausage mixture to the rice and stir. Add the clams to the rice and slightly push them into the paella, then cover again. Once the first clams pop open, add the shrimp in a circular pattern, then recover the pot. Once the shrimp has turned a bright pink color, after 3 to 5 minutes, remove the paella from the stove and stud the paella with the lemon quarters. Serve immediately.

One of the pleasures of summer is gathering with family and friends for what we've always called a crab boil. Most folks, though, call it a Lowcountry boil, and farther north in the Carolinas, it's called Frogmore stew. My favorite way to make it is over an outdoor cooker in a large stockpot with a pull-out colander—that way you can pour out all the goodness onto a newspaper-lined picnic table and everybody can just reach in for a bite. I place little pots of homemade Cocktail Sauce (recipe follows), drawn butter, and lemon wedges all around so guests have easy access for dipping and squeezing.

Gilliard Farms Lowcountry Boil

SERVES 6 TO 8

4½ gallons cold water

2 pints beer

¼ cup Old Bay Seasoning

1 tablespoon crushed red pepper flakes

5 pounds new potatoes, halved

3 pounds Wainright's smoked sausage, cut into 1-inch pieces

1 pound pearl onions

8 ears fresh corn, shucked, silks removed, and cut into thirds

5 pounds whole live blue crabs

5 pounds Wild Georgia shrimp

FILL A 24-QUART steamer pot and punched basket about three-quarters full of water and place over medium-high heat. Add the beer, Old Bay, and crushed red pepper, then bring the seasoned water to a boil. Add the potatoes, sausage, and onions and cook for 10 minutes.

ADD THE CORN and cook for 5 minutes. Then add the blue crabs and cook for 5 more minutes. Add the shrimp and cook for another 4 to 5 minutes, until the crabs have turned bright red and the shrimp have curled and blushed pink.

PULL THE PUNCHED basket out of the pot and let the water drain, then pour the boil over a newspaper-lined table or serve on several large platters.

Cocktail Sauce

MAKES 2½ CUPS

2 cups ketchup

¼ cup lime juice

1 small onion, peeled and roughly chopped

4 garlic cloves, smashed and peeled

2 tablespoons horseradish

1 tablespoon Smokin' Hot 'n' Sweet Seasoning (page 77)

1 teaspoon sea salt

PLACE ALL THE ingredients in a food processor and blend until smooth. Taste and add more garlic, horseradish, or salt to your liking.

What Is the Lowcountry?

Even though there are those who insist the true Lowcountry encompasses only the South Carolina coast and Sea Islands, the case can be made that the Lowcountry stretches from Jacksonville, North Carolina, to Jacksonville, Florida, contiguous with the Gullah Geechee Cultural Heritage Corridor. The land slopes toward sea level through cord grass and pluff mud, and the tides turn twice daily, sometimes by more than nine feet. These marshlands, where freshwater and saltwater meet, are the cradle for the ocean.

Smokin' Hot 'n' Sweet Shrimp and Grits with Vidalia Onion Sausage

Should you prefer the white-table version of shrimp and grits, I offer this version with spicy shrimp bathed in a silky gravy. The sausage is sweetened by Georgia's official state vegetable, the venerable Vidalia onion. A true Vidalia is grown in only 13 counties (and in small portions of 7 others) within south-central Georgia, where the sulfur composition of the soil gives the onion its intense sweetness. The onions are best in season from late April to mid-September.

SERVES 4

1 pound Wild Georgia shrimp, peeled and deveined

1 tablespoon Smokin' Hot 'n' Sweet Seasoning (page 77)

1 teaspoon kosher salt

Juice from 1 lime

4 large sage leaves, roughly chopped

2 sprigs thyme, roughly chopped

1 sprig rosemary, leaves roughly chopped

2 tablespoons pecan oil, divided

2 links Hunter Cattle Co. Vidalia Onion Sausage, cut into ½-inch portions

1 teaspoon all-purpose flour

1 cup heavy cream

CheFarmer's Grits (page 29) for serving

TOSS THE SHRIMP with the seasoning blend, salt, lime juice, sage, thyme, rosemary, and 1 tablespoon pecan oil, making sure they are evenly coated. Set the shrimp aside to marinate for 15 minutes.

HEAT THE REMAINING pecan oil in a large cast-iron skillet and cook the sausage pieces over medium-high heat until they are browned all over and have reached an internal temperature of 155°F, approximately 5 minutes per side. Remove the sausage and set aside.

SAUTÉ THE SHRIMP in the same skillet for 1 minute on each side. Remove the shrimp from the skillet, then sprinkle the flour over the oil and fond (food bits) in the pan and stir, making a light roux. Add the heavy cream to make a quick pan gravy. Once it has thickened for approximately a minute, add the shrimp back into the gravy and cook at least 3 to 4 minutes more, until the shrimp are opaque, pink, and curled.

TO SERVE, SPOON CheFarmer Grits evenly into four bowls. Cover the grits with the shrimp and gravy and sprinkle the top with sausage.

Shrimp and Red Eye Gravy

This is my preferred version of the venerable shrimp and grits recipe, which we didn't actually grow up eating. In fact, I never really thought about it until I was an adult and saw it on menus at five-star restaurants and served in a cream sauce or bathed in beurre blanc. For Saltwater Geechee, shrimp sautéed in a dark roux then ladled over grits or rice was an everyday workhorse meal you ate at breakfast to carry you through a day of fishing, hunting, or plowing. Good Lord, I love me some red eye gravy made from a bit of bacon grease and good, strong leftover coffee. Serve the shrimp and gravy over CheFarmer's Grits (page 29).

SERVES 4

¼ cup bacon grease or unsalted butter

½ cup sweet onion, finely diced

¼ cup all-purpose flour

1 teaspoon sea salt

1 teaspoon chili powder

1 teaspoon sweet paprika

2 cups warm Shrimp Stock (page 100)

1 cup strong black coffee

2 pounds medium shrimp, peeled and deveined

1 teaspoon finely ground black pepper

¼ cup roughly chopped parsley leaves

CheFarmer's Grits (page 29) for serving

PLACE THE BACON grease in a large skillet over medium heat. Once the grease has melted, add the onion and sauté until the onions are translucent, approximately 3 to 5 minutes.

USING A WOODEN spoon or whisk, stir in the flour, salt, chili powder, and paprika and stir until well combined. Continue stirring until the roux starts to turn a deep reddish brown.

ONCE THE ROUX color deepens, stir in the Shrimp Stock to make the gravy. As the gravy begins to thicken, add ½ cup of the coffee. Let the gravy cook over low heat for 18 minutes, stirring frequently to ensure the gravy is thickening and not stuck to the bottom of the pan. Add the remaining coffee, ¼ cup at a time, so that the gravy maintains a smooth consistency.

ONCE THE GRAVY has reached the desired thickness and cooking time, taste it (let it cool on a spoon for a second) for its sweet smokiness and adjust seasonings as needed. Toss the shrimp with pepper, and then add the shrimp in the skillet and cook it in the gravy for 2 minutes, or until the shrimp have curled into commas and turned pink. Remove the skillet from the heat and sprinkle the parsley over the top. Serve with CheFarmer's Grits.

There was a time in the early 20th century when the Georgia oyster industry dominated the world. Descendants of Saltwater Gullah Geechee in their flat-bottomed bateaux harvested the clusters of small, irregular ears for canning, and they carved out decent livings for their families all along the Georgia and South Carolina coast. Industrial pollution caused the collapse of the oyster beds around the 1950s and many of those same fishermen had to go to work for the very mills and factories that destroyed their way of life.

That's not the end of the story, however.

The University of Georgia's Marine Extension service, located on Skidaway Island, has been working to reestablish the Georgia oyster with large single-eared varieties coveted by restaurants and roasters. Because coastal development has been kept to a minimum, we've protected our marshes and wetlands. Wild oyster clusters help to naturally filtrate our waters, and our local oysters are some of the best-tasting ones I've ever eaten. They have the clean, slightly acidic, briny terroir of these intracoastal waterways.

From September through April—the months with an "r" in them—Georgia oysters are ubiquitous on raw bars and at backyard roasts. We begin our Christmas and New Year's celebrations with Hot Tin Oysters, because once those shells pop over the hot fire, it's like unwrapping one of nature's great gifts.

Hot Tin Oysters

TO HOST AN OYSTER ROAST, YOU WILL NEED:

- An outdoor worktable for people to gather around and shuck oysters. A popular and inexpensive configuration is to top two sawhorses with a sheet of plywood, but a long wooden table will do just fine.
- An arsenal of oyster knives. Encourage seasoned shuckers to BYOOK (Bring Your Own Oyster Knife), and provide a range of different knife styles for any guests who don't have their own.
- Alongside a generous supply of paper towels, the typical condiments you'll find on the table are saltine crackers, cocktail sauce, horseradish, lemon wedges, and an array of hot sauces. Just remember: A little goes a long way with these toppings. While cooked oysters do not impart the same delicate taste that you get with raw oysters, it's still worth taking a moment to appreciate them without an overdose of distracting flavors.
- Several sturdy pairs of work gloves. Your best bet is either rubber-coated cotton gloves or stainless steel mesh gloves.
- A roasting pit. You'll need the following to build the pit:
  - Firewood, including kindling
  - Square-point shovel
  - Six cinder blocks
  - A 4-foot-by-2-foot steel sheet, at least ¼ inch thick
  - Two or three burlap sacks
  - Bucket of water
  - And, finally, the oysters—plan for 12 to 24 medium-to-large oysters per person

HOW TO BUILD YOUR ROASTING PIT

DIG A SHALLOW depression about 2 to 4 inches deep in the ground to hold the firewood. Surround the depression with the cinder blocks and set the metal sheet on top.

SOAK THE BURLAP sacks in water. Keep a spare bucket of water within easy reach so that you can keep the sacks wet with each roast.

USE KINDLING TO help get the fire going. Let the fire get hot enough to heat the metal so that a splash of water sizzles and boils off.

SHOVEL A FEW dozen oysters onto the sheet. Since they won't cook evenly if they're stacked in a pile, spread them out evenly across the sheet so that each oyster is in contact with the metal. Cover the oysters with the water-soaked burlap and allow the oysters to steam for 8 to 10 minutes.

THE OYSTERS ARE ready when their shells are just starting to crack open a few millimeters. You'll hear them pop. Just keep in mind that the wider they crack open, the less juicy they will be. Since the oyster's flavorful liquor is one of its most hallowed qualities, it's important not to overcook them.

ONCE THE OYSTERS are done, scoop them up with the shovel and dump them on the table for your guests to shuck and enjoy.

OYSTER PAIRINGS

As for drinks, the traditional libation of oyster roasts is a simple koozie of cold beer. Something light, dry, or even tart can be magical. If you want to preserve the Lowcountry authenticity of your roast, consider the offerings of one of the many craft breweries dotting the Southeastern coast. For a recommendation, see the Spirits entry in the Sources section (page 228) of this book.

If you prefer wine, you can't go wrong with crisp, dry whites such as a sauvignon blanc, Muscadet, or pinot grigio.

Oysters Collarfella

The original Oysters Rockefeller was concocted at Antoine's in New Orleans in the late-1800s. It was named for the richest man in the country, and the oysters were layered with spinach and drenched in butter and breadcrumbs and broiled and . . . well, the rest is history. One day, I started messing around with some oysters from E. L. McIntosh & Son Seafood, one of the local purveyors that is part of the Georgia oyster resurgence. Instead of spinach, I used some leftover Mess o' Greens (page 56) and a wedge of smoky Gouda, and . . . I do believe this appetizer gives Mr. Rockefeller a run for his money.

SERVES 4

2 dozen fresh long-eared oysters, cleaned and shucked

1 cup Mess o' Greens (page 56), slightly pureed

¼ cup smoked Gouda or white Cheddar, shredded

Lemon wedges for serving

Hot sauce for serving

PREHEAT THE OVEN to 450°F.

SET THE OYSTERS, shell side down, on a baking sheet. Top each oyster with a tablespoon of the pureed greens and a teaspoon of the shredded cheese.

PLACE THE PREPARED oysters in the oven and broil them for 6 to 8 minutes, until the cheese is melted and slightly brown. Serve immediately with lemon wedges and hot sauce.

Sapelo Clams Casino

When I returned home to work the farm and as a chef at the Lodge on Little St. Simons Island, the island's naturalist, Stacia Hendricks, introduced me to Captain Charlie Phillips. Captain Phillips runs Sapelo Sea Farms, the oldest clam farm in Georgia. He had brought with him some of his clams and we hopped into the kitchen together and began cooking. I soon discovered that the Sapelo clam is the perfect balance between meat and salt. This dish took us fewer than 10 minutes to pull together and we served it with a good, crusty bread. I'll never forget that day and what a character Captain Phillips is. While we were standing there, he reached into his cooler and pulled out an octopus. "I caught this today, too," he beamed. So we grilled it and ate it, too.

SERVES 2

4 slices bacon, diced

1 small onion, peeled and finely diced

1 cup dry white wine, preferably a pinot grigio or pinot gris

1 teaspoon arrowroot

20 Sapelo Sea Farms clams, rinsed and scrubbed

1 pound cooked linguini

½ bunch culantro (yes, culantro not cilantro), roughly chopped

IN A MEDIUM stockpot over medium-high heat, cook the bacon until it is well done and the fat has rendered. Remove the bacon bits to drain on a paper towel.

ADD THE ONION to the skillet and cook until it has caramelized, 5 to 7 minutes. Add the wine and the arrowroot and stir until all the ingredients melt to create a smooth sauce, 2 to 3 minutes.

ADD THE CLAMS and cover the pot, cooking for 8 minutes. Check to see if the clams have popped open. If not, continue cooking in 5-minute increments until the clams have opened.

DIVIDE THE LINGUINI between two bowls, then top with 10 clams each. Pour the wine sauce over the pasta and clams, then garnish with the culantro and bacon bits.

TIP: *If culantro is hard to find, substitute it with cilantro or flat-leaf parsley. To learn more about culantro, see Smokin' Hot 'n' Sweet Sauce (page 125).*

Fiah / Fire

I guess from the outside, people might have thought we were poor. My daddy worked as a crab boiler and on the docks, my mother was a domestic, and we lived out in the country. But we never went hungry, and I never thought our food was less than. We grew most of it, caught some of it, and hunted wild game and game birds.

Pork was most often on our table because we raised large black hogs on the farm. We kept immaculate pens and we had an old smokehouse. We respected livestock and used the whole hog, from snout to tail, making succulent pulled pork that was slow-roasted overnight and into the next day over wood coals in a pit in the ground. The fat would be rendered into leaf lard and the skin repurposed as cracklin' and rinds—just like the elders taught us.

When I was 10 years old, my dad and great-uncle Horace Jr. gave me a large black hog to raise. Daddy said, "Don't name it. Don't get attached to it. We're raising it for food."

I didn't listen. I fell in love. It was my pet. As that hog grew big enough, I rode bareback across his broad shoulders.

When fall arrived, my dad sat me down and said, "I need you to understand that this is how we survive, how we sustain our family."

As hard a life lesson as it was to learn, I helped put that hog down, clean it, and put it up in the smokehouse. It saw our family through the winter.

The hog roast hearkens back to the ancestors and their ways for slow-cooking tough meats to provide sustenance throughout the winter months. From snout to tail, nothing was wasted.

About once a year, usually around the holidays, we dig a pit, fill it with hot coals, and roast a whole hog. This is a three-day event, my friends, and it is not for the faint of heart. But it is a cause for gathering and provides the most succulent pork for pickin'. Let me walk you through the process, because trust me, it's a process.

Smoked Ossabaw Island Hog (or How to Host a Pig Roast)

FIND A WHOLE HOG

First things first: You'll want to find a 50- to 60-pound hog for a roast.

I am partial to the Ossabaw hog, an heirloom breed with lineage going back to the Canary Islands off the coast of North Africa. Spanish explorers introduced the hogs to the New World back in the 16th century, when they left hogs on Ossabaw Island, a barrier island about 20 miles south of what is now Savannah, Georgia. Ossabaw, once an indigo plantation, was designated a state Heritage Preserve in 1978. Annual public quota hunts help manage the hog population on the island to protect the environment and other endangered resources. Limited off-island breeding programs, including at George Washington's Mount Vernon estate, allow the hogs to be commercially available.

Over time, these foraging and feral hogs developed a high tolerance for salt. This, combined with their ability to store fat during lean months, gives their crimson-colored meat a marbled appearance and a buttery texture similar to the famed Iberico hams of Spain.

You can order one online (see the Sources, page 228), or you can go to a local farm in your area to select a fresh hog. If you order a frozen hog, you'll need to thaw it in an ice cooler for 24 to 72 hours, keeping the temperature consistently cool throughout the thawing time.

FOR THE BRINE

1 gallon hot water

1 gallon apple cider vinegar

12 cups brown sugar

12 cups (three 3-pound boxes) kosher salt

6 cups Jerk Seasoning (page 93)

3 cups smoked paprika

FOR THE HOG

One 50- to 60-pound dressed hog

6 apples, quartered

6 oranges, quartered

6 onions, quartered

4 garlic heads, smashed

12 gallons cold water

Ice

BRINING

ONCE THE HOG is thawed, you'll want to brine it so that the meat will remain moist through the roasting process and the crisped skin will feature a succulent crust.

IN A 5-GALLON bucket, mix together 1 gallon of the hot water with the apple cider vinegar, sugar, salt, jerk seasonings, and paprika until all the solids have dissolved.

PLACE THE DRESSED hog in a 150-quart cooler with a tight-fitting lid. Add the apples, oranges, onions, and garlic. Pour the brining liquid over the hog, then continue to pour cold water on the hog until it is fully submerged, then cover.

KEEP THE HOG submerged for 24 to 36 hours. Periodically add ice to the liquid to keep the hog and the brining solution maintained at below 40°F.

PREPPING THE PIT

WHILE THE HOG is brining, it's time to build your roasting pit. For that, you'll need a shovel, some concrete blocks or bricks, hot coals, burlap sacks, and a large grate or wire mesh (I use the old box springs from a mattress). Alternatively, of course, you could use a roasting box or commercial smoker and grill.

STEP 1. Dig a rectangular pit in the ground at least one foot longer on all sides than the size of your hog. So, if your hog measures 2 feet by 4 feet, you'll dig a pit that's 3 feet by 5 feet and about 3 feet deep.

STEP 2. Line the pit with concrete blocks or bricks.

STEP 3. Fill the surface of the bricks with charcoal briquettes as a starter and heat them up until they turn bright red. Then layer firewood, such as pecan, apple, or oak on top of the briquettes. Burn the firewood down to white hot coals.

ROASTING AND SERVING

Now it's time to prep the hog for roasting.

STEP 4. Once the hog has brined for at least 24 hours, but preferably 36, you will need to prop open the mouth with an apple so that the heat can circulate internally. Then wrap the hog to protect it from direct contact with the heat source. You can wrap it tightly with foil, but wet burlap sacks (even banana leaves) work best. Then set the hog on a large grate or wire mesh.

STEP 5. You're going to need help to set the hog into the pit. Once you have it set over the hot coals, cover the pit and pig with the reserved dirt from the hole.

STEP 6. Every 4 to 6 hours, use a shovel to dig away the dirt on the hog and check its progress. Has the fire cooled too much, and does it need to be stoked? Remember, you want it to roast low and slow, not much more than 250°F consistently over the next 24 to 36 hours. Are the burlap sacks still moist? If not, sprinkle them with water.

STEP 7. At the 24-hour mark, begin checking the internal temperature of the meat with a meat thermometer. Once the thickest part of the meat registers between 155° and 165°F and easily pulls away from the bone, then you're ready to lift the hog out of the pit. Using heavy-duty gloves and another helper, place the whole smoked hog on a long wooden table, unwrap the burlap sacks, and rest the hog for 20 minutes to allow the juices to reconstitute and for it to cool enough to touch.

IN THE MEANTIME, get ready for an old-fashioned pig pickin'. You can let your guests pull their own pork, or you can pull the pork meat straight from the hog and serve it heaped on platters. On another long table, set out slider rolls or hamburger buns, an assortment of barbecue sauces such as CheFarmer's BBQ Sauce (page 124) or Smokin' Hot 'n' Sweet Sauce (page 125), Giardiniera (page 73), Chow Chow (page 76), sliced Vidalia onions, pickle slices, and any other accompaniments you so desire.

How to Make Your Own Pork Rinds (Chicharrónes)

Remove the skin and the fatback from the roasted hog. Render the fatback into a leaf lard that you can use for frying, pastries, and sausages.

Cut the skin into 2-inch pieces. Heat the lard in a large cast-iron skillet until it reaches 350° to 375°F. Drop the skin into the hot oil and fry until golden and crispy. Drain the pork rinds on a paper towel–lined plate. The rinds will be infused with all the flavors from the brine and smoking process, but feel free to salt and pepper to your taste.

Barbecue Sauces

I make two sauces—one tart, the other sweet and spicy—
for slathering, dipping, and dressing pulled pork. Both lend
themselves well to grilled chicken and burgers too.

CheFarmer's BBQ Sauce

MAKES 1 QUART

2 pounds beefsteak
   tomatoes, roughly
   chopped

1 medium sweet onion,
   roughly chopped

4 garlic cloves, peeled and
   roughly chopped

2 tablespoons Jerk
   Seasoning (page 93)

2 tablespoons steak
   seasoning

¼ cup agave nectar

¼ cup apple cider vinegar

1 tablespoon balsamic
   vinegar

1 teaspoon olive oil

PLACE THE TOMATOES, onion, garlic, and jerk and steak seasonings in the bowl of a food processor and cover with the lid. Using the pulse button, blend the ingredients for about 30 seconds. Then pour the nectar and vinegars through the opening, pulsing for 30 seconds after each one. With the processor on high for 2 minutes, pour the olive oil in a slow drizzle, until all ingredients are well combined and smooth.

WARM THE SAUCE in a pan over medium heat to use as a marinade or sauce, or mop it on roasting meats.

Smokin' Hot 'n' Sweet Sauce

MAKES 1 QUART

4 medium tomatoes, roughly chopped

4 African fish peppers, stemmed and seeds removed (see Note)

1 large sweet onion, roughly chopped

1 bunch culantro (yes, culantro not cilantro—see Note) or substitute ½ bunch cinnamon basil and ½ bunch flat-leaf parsley

¼ cup Smokin' Hot 'n' Sweet Seasoning (page 77)

6 garlic cloves

1 tablespoon beef or mushroom broth

¼ cup olive oil

PLACE ALL THE ingredients, except for the olive oil, in the bowl of a food processor and cover with the lid. Using the pulse button, blend the ingredients for about 30 seconds. Then pour the olive oil through the opening while the processor is on high for 2 minutes, until the sauce is well combined.

WARM THE SAUCE in a pan over medium heat to use as a marinade or sauce, or mop it on roasting meats.

TIP: *I love using the Cherokee Purple and Black Prince tomatoes we grow on the farm, because they give this sauce a stunning color. However, feel free to use Roma, beefsteak, and Better Boy tomatoes for your sauce.*

Also, play with your food. Add a tablespoon of teriyaki sauce and use the sauce to baste fish or chicken. Add a splash of harissa to this sauce for extra kick.

NOTE: *The African fish pepper is an heirloom varietal that dates to the 1800s. The delicate plant produces variegated lime-and-cream-colored pepper cones that belie their powerful punch. If you can't find fish peppers, substitute jalapeños for a milder heat or cayenne peppers for a more intense heat.*

NOTE: *Culantro is an herb that looks a little like longleaf lettuce but with sawtooth edges. It has a strong, citrusy note and is most often used in Caribbean and South American dishes. If you can't find it, substitute flat-leaf parsley and cinnamon basil.*

Smothered Pork Chops and Molasses Cornbread

Now that I think about it, I grew up around artisanal butchers like my great-uncle Horace Jr. What folk think of as a craft in cleaving these days—and pay a premium for now—we considered just the way you did things. When we had gone through everything in our smokehouse, we'd go to Southland Market over in Brunswick for our pork belly, or to the Piggly Wiggly, where the butcher would cut a pork chop like a porterhouse steak. One of those, smothered and served over a bowl of rice with a skillet of Molasses Cornbread (recipe follows), could feed the four of us.

SERVES 4

4 center cut pork chops, ½ to 1 inch thick

2 teaspoons pink Himalayan salt

1 teaspoon paprika

1 teaspoon white pepper

1 tablespoon lard, bacon drippings, or butter

1 onion, peeled and diced

2 cups Vegetable Stock (page 34)

1 tablespoon arrowroot

Molasses Cornbread (recipe follows)

RINSE AND PAT the chops dry with a paper towel.

IN A SMALL bowl, combine the salt, paprika, and pepper. Liberally season the chops all over. Set the chops on a plate for 10 minutes.

IN A 10-INCH cast-iron skillet, melt the lard over medium heat. Once the lard has melted, add the chops to the skillet and brown the chops for 2 minutes on each side. Remove the chops from the skillet and set aside, then add the onions to the skillet.

SAUTÉ THE ONIONS until they start to turn brown, approximately 5 to 7 minutes. In a measuring cup or 16-ounce mason jar, make a slurry of the stock and arrowroot.

POUR THE SLURRY over the onions. Stir constantly, and as soon as the gravy starts to bubble, place the chops back into the skillet and reduce the heat to a simmer. Cook the chops for 20 to 25 minutes, while the Molasses Cornbread bakes.

(CONTINUED)

Molasses Cornbread

SERVES 8

2 tablespoons lard, bacon drippings, or butter

1 cup cornmeal

1 cup self-rising flour

½ teaspoon sea salt

1 egg, beaten

¾ cup milk

¼ cup molasses

PREHEAT THE OVEN to 425°F. Place 1 tablespoon of the lard into a medium cast-iron skillet and set the skillet in the oven to melt the lard and heat the pan.

IN A LARGE bowl, stir together the cornmeal, flour, and salt, and make a well in the middle. In another bowl or large measuring cup, mix together the egg, milk, and molasses.

POUR THE WET ingredients into the well of the dry ingredients, then stir the ingredients together until incorporated. You will have lumps.

REMOVE THE CAST-IRON skillet from the oven and pour the cornbread mixture into the skillet. Place the skillet back in the oven and bake for 20 minutes, or until the cornbread is golden brown around the edges and a toothpick inserted in the center comes out clean.

Cracklin' and Red Eye Gravy

The thick layer of marbled fat and meat in the belly of a hog has many uses—bacon being one. Here's one of my favorite ways to use pork belly. You can serve the gravy over biscuits, cornbread, grits, or pork chops.

MAKES 3 CUPS

¼ pound pork belly, cut into thin pieces

1 tablespoon smoked paprika

2 teaspoons kosher salt

½ teaspoon cracked black pepper

½ cup all-purpose flour

3 cups strong coffee, preferably leftover from the morning or day before, more if needed

Molasses Cornbread (page 128) for serving

IN A BOWL, toss the pork belly with the paprika, salt, and pepper. Lay the seasoned pork belly in a single layer in a cold skillet, then place the skillet on medium heat. Allow the fat to slowly render from the pork belly.

ONCE THE FAT has rendered, remove the cracklins and set aside to drain on a paper towel–lined plate.

SPRINKLE THE FLOUR over the fat in the skillet and whisk into a dark roux, approximately 5 to 7 minutes. Add the coffee and let the gravy cook for at least 20 minutes, stirring occasionally. If the sauce thickens too much, add coffee in ½-cup increments.

ONCE THE GRAVY is the right consistency and the flour taste is cooked off, add the cracklins back in and serve hot over Molasses Cornbread.

Calypso Pork Loin and Mango Papaya Sauce

When I ran the Satin and Savory Catering Company in Atlanta, one of my go-to dishes for a large event was sliced pork loin, rather than roasted turkey or prime rib. I also wanted to introduce guests to new and unexpected flavors, like the sunny-spicy-smoky-sweet sensation of Calypso Seasoning, which has a hint of citrus and some heat from dried chilies. When you eat this dish, you'll hear Harry Belafonte singing "Day-O." Serve with a side of Saffron and Coconut Milk Rice (page 30).

SERVES 8

3 pounds pork loin

2 tablespoons Calypso Seasoning (page 149)

1 tablespoon kosher salt

1 tablespoon coconut oil

1 mango, peeled and roughly chopped

1 papaya, peeled and roughly chopped

1 cup Tomato Jam (page 148)

¼ cup Smokin' Hot 'n' Sweet Sauce (page 125)

WITH COLD WATER, wash the pork loin and pat it dry. Let it come to room temperature.

PREHEAT THE OVEN to 375°F.

IN A LARGE bowl, mix the Calypso Seasoning and salt well, then evenly coat the pork loin on all sides with the seasoning.

USING AN OVENPROOF sauté pan on medium-high heat, melt the coconut oil, then place the pork loin in the pan and sear it on all sides. Place the pan in the oven and cook for 30 minutes, or until an internal thermometer inserted into the pork reads 150°F. Allow the pork loin to rest 10 minutes before serving.

WHILE THE PORK loin rests, place the mango, papaya, jam, and sauce in the bowl of a food processor. Turn the processor on high for 1 minute until the sauce is pureed, then pour the sauce into a small saucepan and heat just to a simmer. Slice the pork and spoon the sauce over it.

Cocoa-Rubbed Fillet with Roasted Potatoes

In America, we tend to limit chocolate to sweet treats and do not experiment with its complex versatility in savory dishes. But the ancestors knew better. The mole sauces of Mexico are an amalgam of Spanish and African influences with deep roots in the ancient Aztec culture. One way I like to subvert people's taste buds is to make a deep, smoky, and dark chocolate rub for beef fillets, then sear the fillets to create a light crust that complements the tender meat inside. It's rich and surprising, and often folk wonder if their mouth is deceiving them.

SERVES 4

Four 8-ounce beef fillets

2 tablespoons Cocoa Rub (page 149)

1 pound fingerling potatoes, cut in half

2 tablespoons coconut oil

1 teaspoon smoked salt

½ teaspoon cracked black pepper

PREHEAT THE OVEN to 400°F.

WASH AND PAT dry the fillets. Rub the fillets all over with the cocoa rub, then set aside to come to room temperature.

WHILE THE FILLETS are resting, toss the potatoes in a bowl with 1 tablespoon of the coconut oil, salt, and pepper. Put the potatoes on a baking sheet and place in the preheated oven for 20 minutes. Check for doneness by piercing the potatoes with a paring knife.

WHILE THE POTATOES roast, heat the remaining tablespoon of coconut oil in a cast-iron skillet over medium heat. Add the fillets and sear on each side for 4 minutes. Slide the skillet into the oven and cook for 8 minutes for medium-rare or 12 minutes for medium-well doneness. Serve the fillets alongside the potatoes.

Berbere-Spiced Short Ribs

When I was in culinary school in Falls Church, Virginia, my mentor, David Ivey-Soto, pointed out to me that I had a taste for spices such as mace, nutmeg, and fenugreek. My palate had already traveled farther and wider than the South of my upbringing—those African spices and seasonings were encoded in my DNA. I started rabbit-holing in research, trying to connect with African and Caribbean flavors, trying to find my own voice, find what makes me tick inside a kitchen. That journey led me to this warm, fragrant, and tawny dish. I love eating these ribs with Saffron and Coconut Milk Rice (page 30) or plain old mashed potatoes whipped with sour cream.

SERVES 4 TO 6

4 to 6 pounds beef short ribs, washed and patted dry

½ cup Berbere Spice Blend (page 77)

1 quart beef stock

2 tablespoons olive oil

1 large Vidalia onion, medium diced

4 cloves garlic, peeled and roughly chopped

1 bay leaf

COAT THE RIBS in the Berbere Spice Blend and set aside until they come to room temperature, approximately 30 minutes.

IN A SAUCEPAN, bring the beef stock to a boil over high heat, then turn the heat off. Preheat the oven to 375°F.

IN A CAST-IRON Dutch oven, warm 1 tablespoon of the olive oil over medium-high heat, then sauté the onions and garlic until they soften and have a golden brown hue.

SCRAPE THE ONIONS and garlic onto a plate, then set aside. In the same Dutch oven, heat the remaining olive oil and sear the short ribs two to three at a time and on all sides, approximately 1 minute per side. Place the seared ribs on the same plate as the onions and garlic and repeat until all the ribs are done.

COMBINE THE RIBS, onions, garlic, bay leaf, and hot stock in the Dutch oven, cover, and place in the oven for 2 hours. Remove the cover and continue to cook for another hour until the rib meat is tender and pulls easily from the bone.

Pan-Seared Deer Loin (or Backstrap) with Wilted Glazed Greens

When I was coming up, we always called venison "deer meat," which may be why folks get squeamish about giving it a try. Or they've had venison fattened on corn and grains instead of a natural diet, which makes the meat fatty, instead of giving it the sharp, nutty flavor of wild-raised venison. Or they've had a nice cut of meat that was cooked too long, so it ended up tough and stringy. The key to good venison is medium-rare for the tenderloin, and low and slow for the hardworking roasts. This recipe works well with either the tenderloin or the backstrap.

SERVES 4

One 2-pound deer loin or backstrap

2 tablespoons bacon drippings or butter

FOR THE DRY RUB

¼ cup pink Himalayan salt

1 teaspoon granulated garlic

1 teaspoon granulated onion

½ teaspoon cracked black pepper

½ teaspoon smoked paprika

½ teaspoon ground juniper berries

FOR THE GREENS

1 red pepper, stem and seeds removed, diced

1 bunch scallions, white and green parts thinly sliced

1 pound baby collards, hand-shredded

2 tablespoons apple cider vinegar

1 tablespoon brown sugar

½ teaspoon cayenne pepper

Pinch of kosher salt

RINSE AND PAT dry the loin with a paper towel. Set the loin aside and let it come to room temperature.

WHILE THE LOIN rests, combine the dry rub seasonings together in a medium shallow dish, then roll the loin in the dry rub mixture.

IN A MEDIUM cast-iron skillet or sauté pan, melt the bacon drippings over medium-high heat. Pan sear the loin on each surface for 2 to 3 minutes each, until the whole loin has a nice crust all over and the internal temperature reaches 120° to 135°F. Remove the loin from the pan and place it on a cutting board to rest.

IN THE SKILLET, add in the red pepper and the scallions and sauté for 1 minute, then add the collards and sauté for 1 minute more. Toss in the vinegar, sugar, and cayenne, then sauté for 2 minutes until the greens have wilted and are completely glazed. Sprinkle with a pinch of salt.

TO SERVE, PLACE a bed of greens on a plate. Thinly slice the loin into thin medallions and lay them atop the greens.

STATE OF GEORGIA
1776

UNION SCHOOL
BROOKMAN COMMUNITY

THIS ONE ROOM SCHOOL HOUSE PROVIDED
ELEMENTARY EDUCATION, GRADES KINDERGARTEN
THROUGH EIGHTH, TO THE BROOKMAN COMMUNITY,
FROM THE YEAR 1907 TO 1955.

THIS STRUCTURE IS AN EXAMPLE OF EARLY
AFRICAN-AMERICAN VERNACULAR. IN THE EARLY
YEARS OF THE SCHOOL, ONE OF ITS STUDENTS,
MRS. OPHELIA JOHNSON KILLENS, ATTENDED
KINDERGARTEN THROUGH THE FOURTH GRADE.
MRS. KILLENS HAS BEEN THE SOLE CARETAKER
OF THE SCHOOL SINCE 1955. SOME OF THE PAST
TEACHERS, ACCORDING TO THE TIME FRAME
WERE: ALLIE BALDWIN, GWENDOLYN HANKIN,
ETHEL CHAMBERS, MAMIE HIGHTOWER,
ELIZABETH ROUNDTREE, DONNIE MITCHELL,
MRS. GOLSBY AND DAISY WAYE.

THIS HISTORIC MARKER HAS BEEN DONATED BY
MRS. OPHELIA JOHNSON KILLENS AND WAS
DEDICATED IN THE YEAR OF OUR LORD, 2009.

Deer (Venison) Steaks with Blackberry Sauce

Growing up in the country, we hunted and fished more often than we shopped at a grocery store. From squirrels to rabbits to wild turkeys, we would put up enough meat to feed the extended family. During the winter, we had to keep the deer population down for two reasons: (1) they could destroy our crops, the ones we used to feed our family, and (2) they would starve during the few months when plant growth was dormant. We took only what we needed and used it all, making ground meat for chili or sausages for stews. At the end of spring, we would finally eat the steaks with a sauce made from the wild blackberries that grew along the dirt road.

SERVES 4

- 2 tablespoons pink Himalayan salt
- ¼ teaspoon freshly ground black pepper
- Four 6- to 8-ounce venison steaks, silver skin removed
- 1 pint blackberries
- ¼ teaspoon ground juniper berries
- 1 clove garlic, minced
- ¼ cup aged balsamic vinegar
- ¼ cup molasses
- 2 tablespoons olive oil

COMBINE THE SALT and pepper. Season the steaks all over with at least 1 tablespoon of the salt-and-pepper mixture, and let the steaks come to room temperature, approximately 15 minutes.

WHILE THE STEAKS rest, combine the blackberries, juniper berries, garlic, vinegar, and molasses in a small saucepan and bring to a simmer. Using a potato masher, mash the blackberries. Add 1 teaspoon of the remaining salt-and-pepper mixture and allow the sauce to simmer for 5 more minutes, stirring occasionally to keep it from sticking. Taste the sauce and adjust the seasoning to your particular taste. You may have some salt-and-pepper seasoning left over.

REMOVE THE PAN from the heat and allow it to cool to room temperature, then strain the sauce into a bowl, using a rubber spatula to scrape the sides and slightly mash the sauce through a strainer.

HEAT THE OLIVE oil in a cast-iron skillet just until small wisps of smoke appear, then add the steaks, making sure not to crowd the skillet. Sear the steaks on each side for 3 to 4 minutes, or until the internal temperature of the steaks has reached 135° to 140°F. Remove the steaks from the pan and let them rest for at least 10 minutes. Serve with the blackberry sauce.

Jerk Goat

Funny how when I have traveled abroad and told people I grew up eating deer and goat, they instantly asked me where I was from. When I explained coastal Georgia, I'd get one of two follow-up questions: Georgia has a coast? Or, how country are you? I guess we were pretty country, but I never knew that, because everywhere I traveled and met people from other places, I kept finding commonality through food. Like, I had no idea the seasoning on our goat was considered a jerk seasoning until I tasted jerk chicken the first time. It was like a taste from home.

SERVES 4

4 to 6 pounds goat meat

FOR THE SEASONING

2 cups lime juice

2 bunches scallions, roughly chopped

2 large hot peppers, such as jalapeño

1 sweet onion, peeled and diced

1 bunch cilantro

2 tablespoons apple cider vinegar

2 tablespoons ground allspice

2 tablespoons ground cinnamon

2 tablespoons freshly ground black pepper

2 teaspoons sea salt

2 tablespoons brown sugar

One 3- to 4-inch knob ginger, peeled and chopped

¼ cup honey

WASH AND PAT dry the goat meat and set inside a large bowl or dish.

PLACE ALL THE remaining ingredients except the honey in a food processor or blender and pulse until it resembles a thick rub. Pour three-quarters of the jerk marinade over the goat meat and marinate the meat overnight in the refrigerator.

WHEN YOU ARE ready to grill the goat, prepare your grill and bring the heat to 400°F. Remove the goat from the refrigerator and let it come to room temperature.

PLACE THE GOAT on the grill for a total of 45 minutes, or until the internal temperature reads 165°F, turning the meat halfway through the grilling process.

WHILE THE GOAT grills, heat the reserved one-quarter of the marinade in a small saucepan with the honey. Stir and let the mixture come to a boil. Once it bubbles, remove it from the heat, then serve it as a dipping sauce for the goat meat.

Rabbit Fricassee with Rice Grits

In one of great-grandmother Florine's letters to my Nana, she writes, "I hope your daddy gets me a rabbit for the pot on Easter." When I found that letter, it opened my eyes to the possibilities of putting a rabbit dish on the menu at my former restaurant, The Farmer & The Larder. It sold out that first night and confirmed for me that Southern palates are both exacting and adventurous. Serve the rabbit and sauce with Rice Grits (recipe follows) and roasted rainbow carrots, using the carrot tops as a light garnish on the rabbit.

SERVES 4

- 1 whole 5-pound rabbit, quartered
- 1 tablespoon kosher salt
- 1 teaspoon freshly ground black pepper
- 1 teaspoon Hungarian or sweet paprika
- ¼ cup plus 2 tablespoons arrowroot
- ½ pound thick-cut smoked bacon, cut into lardons (long thin strips)
- 1 medium sweet onion, finely diced
- ¼ pound shiitake mushrooms with stems, roughly chopped
- 2 cups warm Vegetable Stock (page 34)
- 2 cups cooked Rice Grits (recipe follows)
- 2 cups rainbow carrots, roasted and roughly chopped

IN A MEDIUM bowl, cover the rabbit quarters with the salt and pepper, then toss with the paprika and ¼ cup of the arrowroot. Set aside.

IN A LARGE cold skillet, toss in the lardons and turn the heat to medium. It will take about 15 minutes to render the fat off the bacon. Once the fat is rendered, remove the bacon pieces and set them on a paper towel–lined plate to drain.

WHILE STILL SET at medium heat, place the rabbit pieces in the skillet and crisp slightly on all sides for 2 minutes. Remove the pieces and set them on the plate with the bacon bits.

SAUTÉ THE ONION and mushrooms in the skillet until the onions start to turn translucent, 3 to 5 minutes. Add the remaining 2 tablespoons arrowroot and stir to make a quick roux. Add the stock and stir until the arrowroot dissolves. Place the rabbit and bacon bits back into the skillet and cook for 15 minutes. The sauce should slightly thicken.

NOTE: *For our first Easter brunch at The Farmer & The Larder, we served roasted rabbit with mole poblano and called it the Chocolate Bunny.*

(CONTINUED)

Rice Grits

SERVES 4

1 tablespoon unsalted butter

4 garlic cloves, peeled and minced

1 cup rice grits, preferably Congaree and Penn Jupiter Brown Rice Grits

2 cups water

1 teaspoon kosher salt

1 can evaporated milk

1 egg

1 teaspoon hot sauce

1 tablespoon olive oil

1 tablespoon cornstarch

12 ounces Gruyère or smoked Gouda, shredded

IN A MEDIUM heavy-bottomed pan over medium heat, melt the butter, then add the garlic and rice grits. Sauté for 1 minute, making sure the butter has coated the rice grits.

ADD THE WATER and salt to the grits, then bring them to a boil. Turn the heat down to low and let the grits simmer for 15 minutes until the water is almost absorbed.

IN A SMALL bowl, combine the milk, egg, hot sauce, and olive oil and whisk together. In a separate bowl, toss the cornstarch and cheese.

POUR THE MILK mixture into the rice grits and stir until well combined. Add the cheese and stir until the cheese melts completely. Taste and adjust seasonings as necessary. Serve warm with the fricassee.

Porcupines with Marinara

Coming up, this was my favorite dish my mom made and the first dish I ever learned to make. It was also my first lesson in understanding what it means to cook for other people. On the nights my mom had to work late cleaning houses on St. Simons Island, she would leave me the ingredients to make dinner for my little sister, Althea. I would make it the way the recipe was written, but Althea wanted it the way Mom made it—and she would tattle on me for not getting it right. Years later, when I was a young culinary student studying with David Ivey-Soto, he would say that a recipe is just a starting point. Learn the basics then make it your own. Here's my interpretation of Mama's meatballs.

SERVES 4 TO 6

1 pound ground grass-fed beef

1 pound ground pasture-raised pork

1 cup uncooked rice

3 tablespoons Italian seasoning

2 tablespoons garlic, peeled and minced

1 tablespoon Hungarian or sweet paprika

3 teaspoons kosher salt

½ teaspoon freshly ground black pepper

½ cup diced onions, caramelized

One 16-ounce can tomato puree

2 cups water

1 teaspoon crushed red pepper flakes

PREHEAT THE OVEN to 375°F.

IN A MEDIUM bowl, use your hands to combine the ground beef, ground pork, rice, 1 tablespoon of the Italian seasoning, 1 tablespoon of the garlic, paprika, 1 teaspoon of the salt, and pepper.

USING A TABLESPOON, scoop approximately 2 heaping tablespoons of the meat mixture and form into a meatball. Place the meatball in a large cast-iron skillet or deep dish. Repeat until all the meat is used.

IN ANOTHER MEDIUM bowl, combine the remaining Italian seasoning, 1 tablespoon garlic, onions, puree, water, red pepper flakes, and the remaining 2 teaspoons salt. Pour the marinara over the meatballs and place in the oven for at least 20 minutes, or until the meatballs have reached 155°F. The rice will be al dente and stick out of the meatballs like a porcupine's quills. Serve warm.

Farmhouse Burger with Tomato Jam

I used to question my mom's meatloaf, whether I should like that mound of ground beef mixed with bread crumbs and egg as the binder and then shellacked with ketchup. I knew she made it this way to make ground beef go further at mealtime. Yet that old meatloaf came to mind when I was thinking up a recipe for a juicy, out-of-this-world burger. I wanted to put to use the best things from the farm, like late-season tomatoes in a jam, as well as to incorporate a little heat from down island. Serve with roasted purple potatoes, tossed with salt, pepper, and olive oil.

SERVES 8

1 tablespoon pink Himalayan salt

⅛ teaspoon freshly ground black pepper

1 egg

2 tablespoons water

2 pounds ground beef

1 pound ground lamb

1 pound ground chorizo sausage

¼ cup golden flax meal

2 tablespoons Jerk Seasoning (page 93)

4 tablespoons clarified butter or ghee

8 pretzel buns

Tomato Jam (recipe follows)

8 fresh duck or chicken eggs

MIX TOGETHER THE salt and pepper, then in a separate small bowl whisk the egg and water. Set these aside. Combine the ground beef, lamb, chorizo sausage, flax meal, Jerk Seasoning, salt and pepper mixture, and egg in a large bowl. Mix the ingredients with your hands until well combined. Shape the ground meat mixture into 8 burger patties. (I shape my burgers like I did when I was kid. They almost look like a mini round meatloaf, then I slightly flatten them using the palm of my hand.)

IN A LARGE cast-iron skillet over medium heat, melt 2 tablespoons of the butter, then place 4 burger patties in the pan, making sure not to crowd the skillet. Cook the patties 3 to 4 minutes on each side, longer if you desire them well done. Set the patties aside and cover with foil to keep warm, then repeat the process until all the patties are cooked.

SPLIT THE PRETZEL buns. In the same skillet, melt another tablespoon of butter and toast the pretzel buns until golden brown and slightly crisp. Once toasted, slather Tomato Jam on each side of the bun and layer on the burger patty.

MELT ANOTHER TABLESPOON of butter in the skillet, and fry the eggs to your liking in two batches of four. Set one fried egg on each hamburger patty.

(CONTINUED)

Tomato Jam

MAKES 4 CUPS

3 pounds beefsteak
  tomatoes, diced

2 teaspoons olive oil

4 garlic cloves, minced

2 shallots, peeled and
  roughly chopped

1 cup apple cider vinegar

2 teaspoons Dijon mustard

1 tablespoon vindaloo curry
  paste

1 cup honey

½ teaspoon crushed red
  pepper flakes

Sea salt and cracked black
  pepper to taste

IN THE BOWL of a food processor, puree the tomatoes until they are the consistency of a marinara sauce.

IN A HEAVY-BOTTOMED stockpot, heat the olive oil over medium-high heat and sauté the garlic and shallots until caramelized, approximately 7 to 10 minutes.

ADD THE VINEGAR, mustard, curry paste, honey, and red pepper flakes, stirring until just combined. Incorporate the tomato puree and allow the jam to start to bubble. Turn down the heat by half to a simmer and allow the jam to cook for 30 minutes, stirring frequently until it thickens. Remove the jam from the heat. Taste and adjust the seasoning with sea salt and cracked black pepper. When it is to your liking, let the jam cool to room temperature. Store in an airtight container in the refrigerator for up to 2 weeks.

NOTE: *Because we have an 11-month growing season in the Southeastern United States, we get a rolling harvest of tomatoes beginning in late December in Florida and continuing to early June in North Carolina. Georgia tomatoes hit the height of taste during April and May. This versatile jam gets its kick from curry paste, and it is an ideal condiment for grilled burgers and sausages, and as a rub on chicken, lamb, and pork.*

Spices and Seasonings

The spice-and-seasoning blends on this page are taste-shifters, versatile enough to flavor pork, chicken, beef, or fish. The Calypso hints toward the Caribbean and the Cocoa Rub speaks to Mexico and South America—all places where Indigenous, Spanish, and West African cultures melded.

Calypso Seasoning

MAKES ½ CUP

¼ cup dehydrated onion

2 tablespoons holy basil

1 tablespoon oregano

1 tablespoon minced fresh ginger

1 tablespoon ground cinnamon

2 teaspoons pink Himalayan salt

1 teaspoon crushed red pepper flakes

1 teaspoon ground allspice

1 teaspoon honey granules

¼ teaspoon freshly ground black pepper

PLACE ALL THE ingredients in a food processor or spice grinder and pulse for 15 seconds. Store the blend in an airtight container in a cool, dry place for up to 6 months.

Cocoa Rub

MAKES NEARLY 1 CUP

1 tablespoon unsweetened cocoa powder

1 tablespoon pink Himalayan salt

1 tablespoon cracked black pepper

½ tablespoon smoked paprika

½ tablespoon finely ground coffee, preferably Sumatra

PLACE ALL THE ingredients in a sealable plastic bag, mason jar with a lid, or plastic container with a tight-fitting lid. Close and then shake until all the ingredients are well combined. Store in a cool, dry place for up to 6 months.

Win' / Wind

When my parents moved us from Bridgeport, Connecticut, back to the farm in Georgia, we lived for years in the old house that was once the Union School. Once we were old enough, we were given daily chores. Great-grandmother Florine sent my sister, Althea, into the now long-gone chicken coop every morning to gather eggs. Those hens must have smelled her fear, because those yardbirds always wanted to attack Althea, flapping their wings, trying to peck her, coming at her with their talons. They did not like Althea coming in there and shooing them off their nests. You could see the kerfuffle, hear the commotion. To this day, Althea is afraid of chickens.

I love chickens, though, especially the way they each have their personalities. We've got different breeds in our makeshift, free-range chicken pen. The Rhode Island Reds are the most talkative, but the ISA Browns, leghorns, and Orpingtons hold their own. There are a few Braekels and Marans, but the Ameraucanas are our Easter egg layers, leaving little nests of pastel-colored eggs for us to hunt. We do our best to protect them from raccoons and foxes, but snakes are cunning adversaries.

Now that hurricane season is upon us again, I am reminded that I still haven't built a more permanent and protective coop—a Hotel Ameraucanas, if you will—for our yardbirds. One more thing for the never-ending to-do list.

Spatchcock Chicken with Roasted Vegetables

Have I mentioned yet how much I love to cook with cast iron? Cast iron is a beautiful thing—the evenness of the temperature, the telltale char. I love spatchcock chicken almost as much as I love cast-iron cooking, because by laying the bird out, you get consistent surface contact and that GBD (golden, brown, delicious) skin in fewer than 20 minutes. I would rather serve spatchcock chicken than fried chicken—less work, fewer carbs and fats, and all goodness.

SERVES 4

One 5- to 7-pound whole chicken

2 tablespoons sea salt

1 tablespoon salt-free vegetable-pepper seasoning blend

2 sprigs rosemary, leaves removed from stem and roughly chopped

2 sprigs sage, leaves removed from stem and roughly chopped

2 sprigs oregano, leaves removed from stem and roughly chopped

2 tablespoons coconut oil

2 pounds sweet potatoes, skin on, large diced

½ pound Brussels sprouts, cut in half from the stem end

1 large sweet onion, medium diced

2 tablespoons minced garlic

PREHEAT THE OVEN to 425°F. Wipe a 10- to 12-inch cast-iron skillet with olive oil.

WASH AND PAT dry the whole chicken inside and out. Place the chicken on a cutting board breast side down with the neck area facing away from you. Using a sharp and strong pair of kitchen shears, cut from the tail to the neck on one side of the backbone then repeat on the other side until the backbone is easy to remove.

LAY THE CHICKEN out flat and rub the salt and vegetable-pepper seasoning blend generously on the inside of the chicken, then scatter half of the rosemary, sage, and oregano over the inside. Flip over the chicken, breast side up, and rub the skin with 1 tablespoon of the coconut oil. Follow with the remaining salt, pepper, and herbs.

IN A LARGE bowl, toss together the sweet potatoes, Brussels sprouts, onion, and garlic with the remaining coconut oil. Place the vegetables in a single layer in the cast-iron skillet, then set the flattened chicken evenly across the top of the vegetables.

PLACE THE CHICKEN in the oven and roast for 20 minutes or until the thick portion of the chicken registers 165°F and the vegetables are fork-tender. Remove the pan from the oven and allow the juices to redistribute before serving.

Za'atar Roasted Chicken

The Middle Eastern spice blend of za'atar speaks to my soul. The benne seed, carried to this country by my ancestors, forms its foundation. They planted these seeds in secret to provide sustenance and flavor. The sumac grows wild among the woods of Gilliard Farms. The heavy-laden stems bend with beadlike, crimson fruits in a kind of gratitude. The sweet fragrance reaches deep inside of me and conjures a memory that I cannot name.

SERVES 4

FOR THE ZA'ATAR SEASONING

1 tablespoon toasted benne seeds or sesame seeds

1 tablespoon dried thyme

1 tablespoon dried oregano

1 tablespoon ground cumin

1 tablespoon ground coriander

1 tablespoon ground sumac

½ teaspoon kosher salt

½ teaspoon red pepper flakes

FOR THE CHICKEN

One 3½- to 4-pound whole chicken

3 tablespoons za'atar seasoning

2 tablespoons pink Himalayan salt

2 pounds russet potatoes, scrubbed and thinly sliced

2 tablespoons unsalted butter, melted

4 tablespoons olive oil

Freshly ground black pepper

IN A PINT mason jar, combine all the herbs and spices for the za'atar seasoning, cover, and shake until well combined.

WASH AND PAT the chicken dry. Season it inside and out with 2 tablespoons of the za'atar seasoning and 1 tablespoon of the salt. Tie the legs together with kitchen twine and let the chicken sit at room temperature for at least 30 minutes to an hour to allow the seasonings to permeate.

PREHEAT THE OVEN to 425°F. Place a 10-inch cast-iron skillet in the oven.

MEANWHILE, TOSS THE potatoes with the butter, the remaining za'atar and salt, and 1 tablespoon of the olive oil.

ONCE THE OVEN reaches the desired temperature, pull the skillet out of the oven and pour in 2 tablespoons of the olive oil to coat the pan. Layer the potatoes in the pan, creating a nest to hold the chicken.

WITH THE REMAINING 1 tablespoon olive oil, rub down the chicken skin, then set the chicken on top of the potatoes. Place the skillet into the oven and turn the heat down to 400°F. Roast the chicken and potatoes until both are golden brown and crisp and a meat thermometer inserted into the thickest part of the leg meat registers 165°F, approximately 35 minutes.

ONCE THE CHICKEN and potatoes are done, remove the skillet from the oven and let the chicken rest for at least 20 minutes before carving.

Herb Chicken in Goober (Peanut) Sauce

My mom never much talked with me about being a farmer, even when I returned to the farm. Truth is, she never thought I would stay because I had been so emphatic about leaving and never coming back. But now, she shares things with me as we walk and I show her what I'm doing with rotational crops. She points and says, "This was the watermelon patch. Remember, this is where the chicken coop was." Not long ago, we were walking near the woods and she said, "Granddaddy used to grow peanuts right here. He'd run the hogs through here the last months to fatten them up." A mast crop for hogs was just one among George Washington Carver's list of 300 uses for the peanut, which included peanut butter and hair oil. I've got one more to add to his list: this Geechee interpretation of pad Thai. Serve with rice.

SERVES 4 TO 6

One 4- to 6-pound whole chicken, cut into 8 pieces

2 tablespoons dried sage

1 tablespoon dried thyme

1 tablespoon dried oregano

1 tablespoon pink Himalayan salt

2 teaspoons salt-free vegetable-pepper seasoning blend

2 tablespoons bacon grease (or vegetable oil)

1 medium red onion, finely diced

1 bell pepper, finely diced

½ cup creamy peanut butter

2 cups chicken stock

One 13.5-ounce can coconut milk

1 tablespoon fermented hot pepper sauce

2 cups cooked basmati rice

¼ cup unsalted roasted peanuts, chopped, for garnish

1 bunch fresh culantro (yes, culantro not cilantro), roughly chopped, for garnish

WASH AND PAT dry the chicken and place the pieces in a large sealable bag. Combine the sage, thyme, oregano, salt, and pepper seasoning blend in a small bowl, then toss the chicken pieces in the bag with the herbs to coat them all over.

(CONTINUED)

IN A 12-INCH cast-iron skillet, melt the bacon grease on medium heat. Add the chicken pieces and sear all over, about 2 minutes on each side. Once seared, push the chicken pieces to the side of the skillet, then add the onions and bell pepper and sauté just until the onions start to turn translucent, approximately 3 to 5 minutes. Add the peanut butter and stir to coat the chicken.

ADD THE STOCK, coconut milk, and pepper sauce and turn the heat up just until the stock starts to boil, then turn the heat down to a low simmer and cover. Let the chicken cook for 20 minutes or until it reaches an internal temperature of 165°F.

SERVE OVER BASMATI rice and garnish with chopped peanuts and fresh culantro.

TIP: *If culantro is hard to find, substitute with cilantro or flat-leaf parsley. To learn more about culantro, see Smokin' Hot 'n' Sweet Sauce (page 125).*

The Chicken Whisperer

If you google my partner, Jovan Sage, you'll notice that she is a woman of many talents. Herbalist. Activist. Doula. Seed saver. Chicken whisperer.

Yep, you read that right: chicken whisperer.

Once upon a time, a chicken saved Jovan's life. More than a decade ago, when she was traveling the country doing the hard work of electoral organizing, Jovan returned to her then-home of Crown Heights in Brooklyn for a long rest. She baked breads and convinced her landlord to let her build a rooftop garden out of five-gallon buckets and wine crate planters so that she and her neighbors could have easy access to fresh lettuces, scallions, and herbs. She took gardening classes at BK Farmyards and pushed herself to take an urban chicken-keeping class at the food revival space, The Brooklyn Kitchen, after watching a documentary about people and their chickens.

At the time, Jovan was terrified of chickens. So when the instructor invited everyone in the class to hold a yardbird, Jovan had to steel herself when her turn came. The instructor cradled that hen like a delicate football and set it in Jovan's arms, and it was love. Something in Jovan settled and centered in that moment. For the first time in a long time, she felt calm, like she could breathe again.

Thereafter, she became an apprentice at the Imani Community Garden, a place the neighborhood called Fort Hen because of its urban chicken and fresh egg operation. For this largely Black and Caribbean neighborhood, the community garden helped address systemic food apartheid by filling a food desert with wholesome protein and produce options while also connecting kids and their parents with their food's origins. It was transformative.

And now, on Gilliard Farms, Jovan is the chicken whisperer. Our hens trust her, gravitate toward her, and know that she will keep unruly roosters away.

Two-Day Fried Chicken

I need to get real here about fried chicken, because I have a complicated relationship with it. Being defined by where I am from—the South—used to set me off, because I recognized how the region was looked upon as this one thing, this one note. But people elsewhere claimed our food and charged prices that no one ever paid my people, no matter how hard they worked to make the food, while fast food joints devalued the effort, and those shortcuts have long-term consequences for our health and well-being. The reality is we never fried a lot of chicken at home. It's laborious—takes two days to get it right—so it was a treat on special occasions. So when I returned to the coast to work at Little St. Simons Island, I really did not want to include fried chicken on the menu—but visitors come to the South and they want something Southern, and I actually had to learn to make fried chicken as an adult. The time it takes to infuse the chicken with the spices and seasonings and to get that sharp crackle in the crust is so worth it.

SERVES 6 TO 8

DAY 1: THE BATH

Two 4- to-6-pound whole chickens, cut into 8 pieces each

¼ cup pink Himalayan salt

1 tablespoon freshly ground black pepper

¼ cup smoked paprika

2 quarts heavy cream

1 cup fermented pepper sauce

¼ cup lemon juice

WASH AND PAT dry the chicken pieces and set aside.

MIX TOGETHER THE salt and pepper, then combine the mixture with the paprika in a large sealable plastic bag. Place the chicken pieces in the bag and shake to coat them all over with the seasoning.

IN A LARGE glass or ceramic bowl, mix the cream, pepper sauce, and lemon juice until just combined. Remove the chicken pieces from the plastic bag and submerge them in the cream bath. Cover with plastic wrap and set in the refrigerator to marinate for 24 hours.

(CONTINUED)

DAY 2: THE COATING

1 tablespoon pink Himalayan salt

⅛ teaspoon freshly ground black pepper

2 cups arrowroot or all-purpose flour

1 tablespoon garlic powder

Frying oil (peanut, vegetable, avocado, or coconut)

MIX TOGETHER THE salt and pepper. In a large bowl, combine the arrowroot, garlic powder, and the salt-and-pepper blend.

PLACE A COLANDER in the sink and pour the chicken into the colander and allow it to drain for 15 minutes.

FILL A LARGE and deep cast-iron pan or skillet with the frying oil, at least 3 inches deep but no more than halfway up the sides of the pan. Turn the burner to medium-high heat.

WHILE THE OIL heats to 375°F, start coating the chicken pieces with the seasoning blend. Work in stages, coating and frying all the thighs, then all the wings, and so on, so that you don't crowd the pan and get even cooking. Fry the chicken until golden brown and crispy all over and the internal temperature has reached 165°F. Legs, thighs, and wings usually take 13 to 16 minutes. Breasts take a little longer, between 17 and 20 minutes.

TIP: *For the best fried chicken, you'll want to use an older hen that no longer lays eggs. It will have denser meat that can withstand the high heat of frying.*

Nana's Chicken 'n' Dumplings

After a big family celebration, Nana would make a big pot of her chicken and dumplings. She would ladle out these giant bowls just for me and my cousins, then sit and tell us stories about her childhood, about the Union School, or her years as a nurse. This was our time, our comfort, to share with Nana and no one else.

SERVES 8

FOR THE CHICKEN

One 3- to-5-pound whole chicken

2 sprigs oregano

2 sprigs rosemary

16 cloves garlic, peeled and smashed

4 carrots, peeled and diced into ¼-inch cubes

4 celery stalks, sliced ¼ inch thick

2 medium white onions, diced

1 bay leaf

1 tablespoon kosher salt

½ teaspoon freshly ground black pepper

FOR THE DUMPLINGS

1 cup plus 2 tablespoons self-rising flour

1 tablespoon Smokin' Hot 'n' Sweet Seasoning (page 77)

Pinch of sea salt

1 cup buttermilk or heavy cream

WASH AND PAT dry the chicken inside and out. Place the oregano and rosemary sprigs inside the cavity, then place the chicken, garlic, carrots, celery, onions, bay leaf, and salt into a large stockpot and cover with water at least 2 inches above the chicken.

SET THE STOCKPOT on the stove and turn the heat to high. Once the water comes to a boil, turn the heat to low and let the chicken simmer for an hour. Periodically skim the top of the chicken stock with a large spoon to remove any scum.

AFTER 1 HOUR, remove the chicken and the bay leaf. Discard the bay leaf, then remove the skin and debone the chicken. Discard the carcass and roughly chop all the chicken meat before returning it to the stockpot. Taste the broth and adjust the seasoning with salt, pepper, or more herbs.

IN A MEDIUM mixing bowl, stir together the flour and seasonings for the dumplings. Slowly stir in the buttermilk until all the ingredients are well combined but not overworked.

BRING THE STOCK, meat, and vegetables back to a rolling boil over medium-high heat. Using a tablespoon, drop chunks of dumpling dough into the stock. Once all the dumpling dough has been used, turn the heat down to low and simmer for 5 minutes.

IF THE CHICKEN and dumpling sauce is not thick enough for your liking, you can add a mixture of 2 tablespoons arrowroot or cornstarch and 2 tablespoons warm water in increments until you achieve the desired thickness. Ladle the dish into a big bowl and breathe all that goodness in. It'll make everything all right.

When I came back home in 2011, I promised myself that for the rest of my life I would not cook on Thanksgiving. After having worked in hotels and in catering for most of my time as a chef, I had not had the holiday off in years. After four days of preparation, by the time the holiday rolled around I could not enjoy the celebration. But my dad came to me and told me it was my turn to cook. "You're doing this for the family," he said. All right, I thought, but on my terms. I bought a fresh turkey, brined it, injected it, then fried it. Aside from a little day-before prep, most of the day-of prep and cooking can be completed within four hours. Now, it's tradition and we all get to enjoy the day.

Herb Fried Turkey with Barnyard Oyster Dressing

Along the Southeastern coast, we celebrate the holidays outdoors. The heat and humidity subside, the skies turn a brilliant shade of blue, and we gather around backyard fires with family and friends. Thanksgiving falls in the middle of oyster season, when they are in their prime: all briny and cold. So set up your Hot Tin Oysters (page 109) and save a few for the dressing.

SERVES 12

FOR THE TURKEY

One 20-pound fresh turkey

4 carrots, peeled and roughly chopped

4 celery stalks, roughly chopped with the leaves

3 medium onions, peeled and roughly chopped

1 cup olive oil

½ cup (1 stick) unsalted butter

¼ cup Italian seasoning, finely ground

2 tablespoons garlic powder

2 tablespoons onion powder

1 tablespoon pink Himalayan salt

4 sprigs rosemary

4 sprigs sage

4 sprigs thyme

FOR THE BRINE

5-gallon bucket

1 cup kosher salt

1 cup brown sugar

2 cups hot apple cider

Water to cover

WASH AND PAT dry the turkey, inside and out. Remove the giblets from the turkey cavity and place them in a pot with half the carrots, celery, and onions. Cover with water and let simmer for 3 hours to create a giblet stock.

IN A SMALL saucepan, combine the olive oil, butter, Italian seasoning, garlic and onion powders, and salt. Turn the heat to low until the butter melts, then remove it from the stove. Using an immersion blender, blend the butter mixture for 1 to 2 minutes.

STUFF THE CAVITY of the turkey with the rosemary, sage, and thyme, then truss the turkey. Using a turkey injector, inject each breast with the butter mixture in at least four places. Do the same with the thighs and legs until you've used up all the butter mixture. Place the turkey in a clean 5-gallon bucket with the brining liquids and pour in enough cold water to fully cover the turkey. Place the turkey in the fridge overnight.

ONCE THE GIBLET stock is done, set it aside to cool to room temperature. Remove the giblets and the neck from the stock, picking the meat and discarding the bones. Divide the stock, reserving one cup for the dressing and the remainder with the meat for the gravy. Store both in the refrigerator overnight.

(CONTINUED)

A Few Words about Deep-Frying a Turkey

- Do not attempt to fry a frozen turkey or one that is just partially thawed. A fresh turkey works best.
- Wear protective clothing: long pants or jeans, closed-toe leather shoes, a long-sleeved shirt, and garden gloves or leather work gloves.
- Always keep a working fire extinguisher nearby. If you start a grease fire, use sand or baking soda to suffocate the flames.
- Keep children and pets away from the cooking area, which should be in an open area—never on a wooden deck or inside a garage or carport.
- Never leave the hot oil or the frying turkey unattended.
- Always use the turkey stand and retriever hanger that came with your turkey-frying kit.
- Use a long-stemmed thermometer to keep track of the oil's temperature. Heat the oil to a temperature between 350° and 375°F, approximately 30 minutes. The best oils to use: peanut or canola. When your oil reaches the desired temperature, slowly lower the turkey into the turkey fryer, making sure not to splatter or tip over the fryer. The oil temperature will drop at first but it will return to the desired range. The lowest temperature for it to ignite, is 412°F, so it is important to maintain the temperature between 350° and 375°F.
- The turkey is finished frying when its skin is crisp and the internal temperature in the thickest part of the meat not next to a bone reaches 175°F, approximately 30 minutes to 1 hour, depending upon the size of the bird.
- Let the turkey rest for at least 15 minutes prior to slicing.

ABOUT AN HOUR before you are ready to fry the turkey, pull it out of the brining liquid, rinse, and pat the turkey dry. Set it aside to allow it to get to room temperature. Following the manufacturer's directions, fry the turkey (see previous page).

Barnyard Oyster Dressing

SERVES 12

1 pound smoked bacon, diced

1 pound shucked oysters, roughly chopped with liquid reserved

One 12-ounce can evaporated milk

1 cup giblet stock, reserved from Herbed Fried Turkey (page 167)

2 eggs

4 stalks celery, thinly sliced

1 large onion, diced

4 cups cornbread cubes

4 cups stale bread cubes

1 teaspoon sea salt

1 teaspoon freshly ground black pepper

PREHEAT THE OVEN to 375°F. Butter a large cast-iron pan or baking dish.

IN A SEPARATE large skillet, cook the bacon until the fat is rendered. Remove the bacon to a paper towel–lined plate to drain. In a medium bowl, combine the reserved bacon grease with the oyster liquid, evaporated milk, giblet stock, and eggs, and pulse with a hand blender for 30 seconds.

IN A SEPARATE large bowl, combine the bacon, oysters, celery, onions, cornbread and bread cubes, salt, and pepper. Stir until well combined. Pour half of the liquid mixture over the dry mixture and toss. Continue adding liquid in ¼-cup increments until the dressing is moist but not soggy or soupy.

TRANSFER THE DRESSING to the prepared baking dish without trying to pack it all in if you have more than it can hold. Butter a second dish if necessary. Place the dish(es) in the oven for 45 minutes, or until it is golden brown on top and cooked all the way through. It should still be tender and moist, not dry and crumbly. By the time the dressing is finished the turkey will be almost done.

FOR THE GIBLET GRAVY

POUR THE RESERVED giblet stock and meat into a medium saucepan. With an immersion blender or whisk, mix 1 tablespoon arrowroot or cornstarch into the giblet stock. Heat the stock over medium-low heat and stir as it warms and thickens. Once it has reached the desired consistency, remove from the heat and pour the gravy in a boat for serving.

Roasted Squab with Three Sisters Succotash

There are so many dishes we don't try because we think they are too fancy, too exotic, or out of our reach, simply because it's not something we've tried before—or it's a rustic dish common to country folk but served to city folk in a white-tablecloth restaurant for a high price tag. I've seen that scenario played out so often, especially with yardbirds and game birds I've taken for granted down on the farm. But I'm here to encourage you to be adventurous in the kitchen. This dish is ideal for autumn when there are rolling seasons for game birds, from pheasant and grouse to quail and woodcock. I've built this recipe around squab, which is really just pigeon. But this recipe is adaptable to any game bird, and it pairs so well with the things that are in season.

SERVES 4

4 squab

2 tablespoons kosher salt

1 tablespoon salt-free vegetable-pepper seasoning blend

1 tablespoon ground sumac

½ cup (1 stick) unsalted butter, melted

1 cup fresh corn, cut from the ear and blanched

1 cup Sea Island Red Peas

1 cup crookneck squash, diced

½ cup sliced scallions

PREHEAT THE OVEN to 400°F. Line a half sheet pan with parchment paper. Wash the squab under cool water, then pat dry.

COMBINE THE SALT, pepper blend, and sumac, then rub the seasonings all over the squab, inside and out.

SET THE SQUAB on the prepared sheet pan, douse them with the melted butter, then roast them in the oven for 20 minutes or until the internal temperature reaches 135°F.

REMOVE THE SQUAB from the oven and strain off the fat from the sheet pan into a medium skillet. Turn the heat to high and sauté the corn and peas until hot. Add the squash and scallions and toss in the pan until the vegetables are mixed well. Cook for 1 minute more, then taste to adjust the seasonings. To plate, create a nest of the succotash and set the squab in the center.

Rose Petal Quail

Nana loved her roses: deep pink American Beauties, peachy Indian Femmas with ruffled fuchsia tips, big white Moondance Floribundas, coral-shaded Tropicanas, vibrant-yellow Harrisons fit for any Texan, and so on. She tended them as lovingly as she did all her children and grandkids, and they bloomed just as brightly throughout the year in stages of color bursts. We just planted 21 different varieties of rosebushes on the farm in honor of her. You can bet those first fragrant blooms have found their way into this dish, which pairs perfectly with Gullah Rice (page 33).

SERVES 4

FOR THE ROSE AND PRICKLY PEAR SYRUP

1 cup organic rose petals

1 cup water

4 large prickly pears, peeled

¼ cup honey

1 teaspoon ground cinnamon

¼ teaspoon ground nutmeg

FOR THE QUAIL

2 tablespoons pink Himalayan salt

¼ teaspoon freshly ground black pepper

8 quail, cleaned and split

2 tablespoons unsalted butter

4 garlic cloves, peeled and smashed

½ cup pinot grigio

½ cup chicken stock

Rose petals for garnish

STEEP THE ROSE petals in the water in a small covered saucepan over medium-low heat. Allow the rose petals to simmer until they lose color, approximately 30 to 40 minutes.

STRAIN THE ROSE water and allow it to cool to room temperature. Reserve ¾ cup and store the remaining rose water in an airtight container in the refrigerator for up to 2 weeks.

IN A SMALL saucepan, combine the ¾ cup rose water, prickly pears, honey, cinnamon, and nutmeg and simmer over medium-low heat for 15 minutes. Strain the syrup through a fine mesh while mashing the prickly pears.

ONCE THE ROSE and Prickly Pear Syrup is ready, mix together the salt and pepper. Lightly season each quail with the salt-and-pepper mixture.

IN A LARGE skillet, melt the butter with the garlic cloves on medium-high heat. Once the butter has stopped foaming, sear the quail on each side, then set the quail aside on a separate plate.

TO THE SKILLET, add the wine, syrup, and chicken stock and let it come to a simmer. Return the quail to the skillet, cover and cook for another 5 minutes. Garnish with rose petals.

NOTE: *If you do not have organic rose petals readily available, substitute 1 cup of food-grade rose water.*

Dark Wing Duck with Almost Rum Orange Glaze

This recipe was inspired by a chef, a syrup, and a comic. Stay with me here. Friend and fellow Culinary Institute of America alum Brandon Walker, now the chef-owner of Essie's Restaurant in Poughkeepsie, New York, used to make this fried duck wing shellacked with an orange glaze that was out of this world. The taste of it has stayed with me in the best possible of ways. Fast forward a decade, when I had my own restaurant, and the owners of Richland Rum gifted me a bottle of their Almost Rum cane syrup. I knew exactly what I wanted to do with it. Now something a lot of people don't know about me is that I am a huge comic book fan—I used to devour them as a teenager and can still lose a few hours in a comic book store. One of my more recent favorites is the character Darkwing Duck, the superhero alter ego of a suburban dad and a bit of a pulp-inspired parody. My version of Brandon's wings isn't so much a parody as an homage.

SERVES 6 TO 8

FOR THE WINGS

4 pounds duck wings

2 tablespoons melted butter

1½ cups coconut vinegar

½ cup lime juice

¼ cup gochujang sauce

Frying oil of choice (peanut, vegetable, coconut)

Thin spears of rainbow carrots for garnish

FOR THE RUB

1 tablespoon Smokin' Hot 'n' Sweet Seasoning (page 77)

2 teaspoons garlic powder

1 teaspoon ground cinnamon

1 teaspoon ground rosemary

1 teaspoon ground thyme

1 teaspoon ground ginger

½ teaspoon ground cloves

FOR THE ALMOST RUM ORANGE GLAZE

½ cup pure cane syrup, such as Richland Rum's Almost Rum

1 cup fresh-squeezed orange juice

PREHEAT THE OVEN to 300°F and line a baking sheet with parchment paper. Wash and pat dry the duck wings, then place them in a large bowl.

IN A SMALL bowl, combine the Smokin' Hot 'n' Sweet Seasoning with the garlic powder, cinnamon, rosemary, thyme, ginger, and cloves. Toss half of the rub mixture with the duck wings, then pour the melted butter over the wings, tossing again to make sure all the wings are coated. Set the wings in a single layer on the prepared baking sheet and parbake them in the oven for 2 hours.

WHILE THE WINGS are in the oven, mix the remaining half of the spice mixture with the vinegar, lime juice, and gochujang sauce. Divide the vinaigrette in half between a large bowl and another container.

ONCE THE WINGS have finished parbaking, remove them from the oven and let them cool. Once they are cool enough to handle, put the wings in the large bowl with the vinaigrette, cover with plastic wrap, and place in the refrigerator (along with the reserved vinaigrette) to let the wings marinate for 2 hours.

ONCE YOU ARE ready to finish the wings, remove them from the refrigerator. Pour them into a colander in the sink and allow them to drain and come to room temperature, approximately 15 minutes. While the wings rest, set a deep skillet on the stove and fill it halfway with your frying oil. Turn the heat to medium and let the oil get to 375°F.

ONCE THE WINGS have drained and the oil has reached the desired temperature, fry the wings in batches (so as not to overcrowd the pan until the skin is crispy, approximately 3 to 5 minutes per batch). Set the wings on a paper towel–lined plate until ready to serve.

TO MAKE THE orange glaze, in a small saucepan, combine the reserved vinaigrette, the cane syrup, and the orange juice and bring to a simmer over low heat for 10 minutes, stirring occasionally until all the syrup is dissolved.

SERVE THE WINGS with the orange glaze and carrot spears.

Georgia Benedict

If great-grandfather Horace wasn't making fish and grits, then great-grandmother Florine was making a biscuit sandwich with an egg and bacon. That was our breakfast on the go, and it's still one of my favorites. When I became a chef and worked in hotel kitchens, I had no choice but to become an expert in dishes like Eggs Benedict, and here I put my own Gilliard Farms spin on it. It's just a fancy way of serving Florine's bacon-and-egg biscuit.

SERVES 6

6 pork belly strips, sliced ½ inch thick

12 poached eggs

1 tablespoon vinegar

FOR THE TOMATO JAM HOLLANDAISE

4 egg yolks

1 tablespoon Tomato Jam (page 148)

Pinch of kosher salt

½ cup (1 stick) hot melted butter

FOR ASSEMBLY

6 Hot Buttermilk Biscuits (page 45), split in half and toasted

½ bunch parsley, chopped with no stems

PREHEAT THE OVEN to 400°F. Line a baking sheet with foil, folding it over the edges of the pan. Lay the pork belly strips about 1 inch apart on the pan and place the pan in the oven for 40 minutes. Flip the pork belly strips at the 20-minute mark so that they are crisped on both sides. Remove the pork belly from the oven and set them on a paper towel–lined plate to drain and cool slightly.

WHILE THE PORK belly cools, poach the eggs. My advice: use the freshest possible eggs you can find—straight outta the coop, if possible. Crack each egg into its own small ramekin or saucier.

FILL A DEEP skillet about halfway up with water and add the vinegar. Bring the water to a boil over high heat.

TURN OFF THE heat and stir the water, then gently add 6 of the eggs and cover for 2 to 3 minutes. Remove the eggs with a slotted spoon and set on a paper towel–lined plate. Turn the heat back on high and bring the water back to a boil and repeat the process with the remaining 6 eggs.

ONCE THE EGGS are poached, quickly make the Tomato Jam Hollandaise.

PLACE THE EGG yolks, jam, and salt into a blender and pulse. Turn on the blender to the medium setting and slowly drizzle in the hot butter until the yolks start to emulsify. Taste and adjust the seasonings accordingly.

TO ASSEMBLE: PLACE an open-faced toasted biscuit on six plates. Cut each pork belly strip in half and set a piece on each biscuit half. Top each biscuit with a poached egg, then spoon on generous portions of the Tomato Jam Hollandaise. Garnish with the chopped parsley.

TIP: *If you want to give your brunch a distinctly coastal Georgia accent, substitute crab cakes for the pork belly using the recipe for Crab Diablo (page 97). You can also give the Tomato Jam Hollandaise an extra zip by adding a teaspoon of Dijon mustard.*

Nana's Egg Pie with Breakfast Potatoes

Nana made a quiche about once a week, but she never called it that. It was an egg pie to her, and whether it's called a quiche, a frittata, or a strata—it will always be an egg pie to me. The secret to this pie is twofold: its freshness and its utility. In the spring, when we have an abundance of eggs because as the days get longer the hens lay more and the spring vegetables come in quicker than we can pick them, this recipe makes the most of the bounty of our farm. This egg pie also offers a great way to use up the ends of bread.

SERVES 6 TO 8

FOR THE EGG PIE

Olive oil spray

1 teaspoon pink Himalayan salt

1 teaspoon salt-free vegetable–pepper seasoning blend

1 dozen large eggs

2 cups coconut cream

4 cups stale bread, cut into cubes

2 cups spinach leaves, roughly chopped or torn

1 large (½ cup) portobello mushroom cap, sliced

1 small onion (½ cup), finely diced

1 bell pepper (½ cup), seeded, stemmed, and diced

2 jalapeño peppers (¼ cup), seeded, stemmed, and diced

1 tablespoon basil, roughly chopped

1 tablespoon flat-leaf parsley, roughly chopped

1 cup crumbled feta

2 Roma tomatoes, sliced

FOR THE POTATOES

3 Yukon Gold potatoes, medium diced

1 tablespoon olive oil

1 tablespoon minced garlic

½ bunch scallions, white and green parts finely sliced

PREHEAT THE OVEN to 375°F and line a baking sheet with parchment paper. Spray the bottom and sides of a 3-quart baking dish or a 10-inch cast-iron skillet with olive oil.

IN A SMALL bowl, mix together the salt and vegetable-pepper blend. In a large bowl, whisk together half of the salt-and-pepper combination with the eggs and cream.

(CONTINUED)

GENTLY FOLD IN the bread cubes, spinach, mushrooms, onions, peppers, basil, parsley, and ½ cup of the feta into the eggs. Pour the egg pie mixture into the prepared dish or skillet, then top with the remaining feta and the tomatoes.

LET THE EGG pie sit for 15 minutes. While the egg pie rests, toss the potatoes with the olive oil, garlic, and remaining salt and pepper mix. Place the potatoes on the prepared baking sheet, then place both the egg pie and the potatoes into the preheated oven and bake for 20 minutes. After 20 minutes, turn the egg pie 180 degrees and cook for 20 minutes more, until the egg pie is firm and golden. The potatoes should be browned and fork-tender.

REMOVE THE EGG pie from the oven and let it rest 5 minutes before serving. In a medium bowl, toss the cooked potatoes with the scallions. Serve the egg pie and potatoes together.

TIP: *I use a combination of sourdough and brioche breads for the cubes.*

TIP: *You can make the egg pie a day ahead. Cover the uncooked egg pie with plastic wrap and place it in the refrigerator overnight. Remove the egg pie at least 15 to 20 minutes before you pop it into the oven to allow it to come to room temperature. Then bake it as directed.*

Sweet'n / Nectar

While writing this book, for inspiration I returned time and again to the women in my life—Florine, Ophelia, Effie, Mary Lou, Edna, Jessica, and Alice—who influenced me in the kitchen. I still make Nana's Sweet Potato Pie (page 200) every chance I get. And the hulking cast-iron sugarcane press stamped MADE IN SAVANNAH that my great-grandmother and great-grandfather received as a wedding present rests on the farm near the chicken coop. I want to get it working again to make my own cane syrup and to help revive a line of purple ribbon sugarcane that once grew thick on Sapelo Island.

But I would be remiss if I did not honor my father, who showed me how good food is also a form of fine art.

My mother made the biscuits, but my father—my father—made French pastries. He could not read or write until the age of 25, but he had a trade as a baker. Coming up in Bridgeport, Connecticut, he learned through sight and practice how to take his time to make golden croissants that delicately shattered, apple turnovers that sent flakes down the front of your shirt, and cookies with the perfect balance of crisp-tenderness, which, now that I think about it, describes him in a lot of ways. Because he was denied practicing his trade as a Black man in the South in the 1970s, he was afraid I would never be able to lead my own kitchen, so he discouraged even the notion of my becoming a chef.

Today, during those moments when we sit around the table sipping on coffee, he says that if he knew then what he knows now, he would have encouraged me go to culinary school right out of high school. But we've all got our journeys, right? And maybe this one wouldn't be as sweet had it been so easy.

Effie's Brown Sugar Molasses Pound Cake

I called my mom to ask her about her molasses pound cake, and she was like, "Nobody wants that recipe. That's just an ol' cake we made for family." No one, though, had ever written down the recipe, so sometimes it was made with brown sugar, sometimes molasses. So I asked my sister, Althea, and she was telling me how she makes it with fresh lemon juice. It is a versatile pound cake that you can adapt for the seasons, but my favorite way to make it any day of the year is with a combination of brown sugar and molasses, which gives it a rich amber color and a deep caramel flavor. I serve it with fresh whipped cream and whatever fruit is in season.

SERVES 8

1½ cups (3 sticks) unsalted butter, room temperature

2 cups firmly packed brown sugar

½ cup molasses

7 eggs

3 cups all-purpose flour

PLACE A RACK in the middle of the oven and preheat the oven to 375°F. Lightly butter and flour a Bundt or angel food tube pan.

IN THE BOWL of a stand mixer with a paddle attachment, cream together the butter and sugar on medium-high speed until pale and fluffy, approximately 5 minutes. With the mixer still running, stream in the molasses and beat for 1 minute more.

ADD THE EGGS one at a time, beating the cake batter after each one until fully incorporated. After all the eggs are incorporated, turn off the mixer and scrape down the sides of the bowl with a spatula.

TURN THE MIXER to low and add the flour. Once the flour has settled into the batter, increase the speed to medium and beat the batter for 2 more minutes.

TURN OFF THE mixer and tap the paddle attachment on the side of the bowl to release as much of the batter back into the bowl. Using the spatula, give the batter one or two more stirs to make sure all the ingredients are incorporated.

(CONTINUED)

POUR THE BATTER into the prepared cake pan. Tap the pan two or three times on the counter to get rid of any air pockets. Bake the cake for 30 minutes, then check doneness with a toothpick in two to three places. If it's not quite done, bake 10 to 15 minutes more. Once done, remove the cake from the oven and set the pan on a wire rack to cool. Let the cake come to room temperature in the pan. Run a knife around the edges to loosen, then invert a cake plate on top of the pan. Using both hands, flip the cake pan over so that the cake slides easily from the pan onto the plate.

Strudel with Almost Rum Syrup

I'll never forget this moment sitting in a Western Studies class in college. The professor challenged the class to identify their Western European heritage, then he went student by student, asking for their answers. But he ignored me. I raised my hand and said, "You didn't ask me." He laughed and the class nervously laughed with him. "My great-grandmother on my father's side was German," I said. There was an audible gasp. But I understood that my connection to my German heritage ran deep and authentic. When I was stationed in Germany, I went all in on the local fare, falling in love with schnitzel and the quick breads. So, when I became a chef, I decided to embrace all the parts of me and my history. This recipe is a marriage of a traditional Southern biscuit and a Bavarian pastry.

SERVES 8 TO 10

FOR THE STRUDEL

2¼ cups self-rising flour

1 teaspoon ground cinnamon

¼ teaspoon (a pinch) of fine sea salt

2 cups heavy cream

1 cup light brown sugar, firmly packed

FOR THE ALMOST RUM SYRUP

1 cup Richland Rum's Almost Rum or other pure cane syrup

2 tablespoons unsalted butter

¼ teaspoon freshly grated or ground nutmeg

PREHEAT THE OVEN to 375°F and line a baking sheet with parchment paper.

COMBINE 2 CUPS of the flour, cinnamon, and the salt in a bowl. Add the heavy cream to the flour mixture and stir until the dough starts to take on a tacky consistency (where the dough barely sticks to your palm when you lay it on top of the dough).

USING HALF OF the remaining flour, dust the countertop and turn the strudel dough onto the floured surface. Using a rolling pin, roll the dough to a ¼-inch-thick rectangle, then sprinkle the brown sugar across the surface of the dough. From one of the long sides, roll the dough lengthwise into a cigar shape, pinching the ends of the dough together and along the seam. Use a touch of water to your fingertips to seal it.

WITH A SHARP knife, slice the strudel roll into 2-inch sections and place on the prepared baking sheet. Place the baking sheet in the heated oven and bake for 10 minutes. Turn the sheet halfway and bake for 5 minutes more. Test the strudel for doneness by inserting a knife into the dough. If it comes out clean, the strudel is done. If not, bake 5 minutes more.

WHILE THE STRUDEL is baking, make the Almost Rum Syrup. In a small saucepan over low heat, stir the Almost Rum, butter, and nutmeg together using a whisk until the butter melts and all the ingredients are integrated.

DRIZZLE ALMOST RUM Syrup over the strudel, then serve warm and enjoy. Remember to share. These are so good, you may not want to, but share like your mama taught you.

Blackberry Doobie

I call the woods around the farm Where the Wild Things Are, because great-grandmother Florine's mimosa trees and great-grandfather Horace's blackberries and muscadines have all volunteered and gone a little crazy back in there, where they are free to flourish. As a kid, we had wild blackberries growing along the edges of the ditch when Galilee Road beside our farm was a dirt road. When they were ready for picking, my cousins and I would fill our buckets with more blackberries than Nana could possibly use because we knew if we did, she would say, "Now, y'all done picked enough for to make a doobie." A doobie is kind of like a cobbler, but it's more akin to sweet dumplings. Serve warm with fresh whipped cream, vanilla bean ice cream, or a scoop of one of the gelatos on page 211. Once you take a bite, you'll taste summer for real.

SERVES 8 TO 10

4 pints blackberries

½ cup Sucanat or granulated sugar

2 tablespoons arrowroot or cornstarch

1 cup cold water

4 tablespoons cold butter

½ batch Hot Buttermilk Biscuits dough (page 45)

IN A LARGE pot, toss the blackberries with the sugar and arrowroot. Let the blackberries sit for 20 minutes, then add the water and butter and turn on the heat to medium. Once the blackberries come to a boil, turn the heat down to simmer.

WHILE THE BLACKBERRIES simmer, use a tablespoon to drop biscuit dough onto the surface of the blackberries until you've used up all the dough. Cover the pot and cook for 15 to 20 minutes, until the dough is cooked through.

NOTE: *Sucanat is simply a less-processed derivative of natural sugarcane and involves no chemicals in the making the way white granulated sugar does. The gift: a healthier sweetener with a richer, more complex flavor profile, which means you need less of it in a recipe.*

Magic Cobbler

When my mom first let me start making desserts, she taught me how to make this cobbler with canned peaches. I thought it (and I) was the bomb because of how crusty and juicy it turned out. So, when I went picking blackberries, I asked my mom if I could try this recipe with them. She was straight up excited I had taken the initiative. By the time I became a chef, her cobbler recipe was my quick dessert go-to. This recipe calls for fresh blackberries, but feel free to substitute strawberries, blueberries, peaches, or a mix of summer fruits. Serve warm with a side of ice cream and feel the magic.

SERVES 6 TO 8

- 1 cup (2 sticks) unsalted butter
- 2 cups fresh blackberries
- ½ cup granulated sugar
- 2½ cups self-rising flour
- 2 cups whole milk

PREHEAT THE OVEN to 350°F. Place the butter in a deep 9-by-11-inch pan and put it in the oven to melt the butter.

IN A MEDIUM saucepan, combine the blackberries and ¼ cup of the sugar and turn the heat to medium, stirring for 2 to 3 minutes or just until the sugar melts. Remove the pan from the heat.

IN A MEDIUM bowl, mix together the flour, remaining ¼ cup sugar, and milk to create a thick batter.

REMOVE THE CAKE pan from the oven and pour in the batter and spread it out to the corners. Pour the blackberries evenly over the batter, then pop the pan back into the oven to bake for 25 minutes, or until a toothpick comes out clean. Continue to bake in 5-minute intervals until the cobbler is done.

J-E-L-L-O Pie

Whenever I came home on leave from the Army, my Aunt Mary Lou
would call my name through the woods from the other side of the farm:
"Matthew!" She had this commanding voice, so I would head straight over
and she would have this pie waiting for me—whether I was visiting for four
hours or four days. She's been gone eight years now, and I've been trying
to figure out how to replicate this humble pie that she always made just
for me. I'm not entirely sure I've done it here, but I'm also not sure there's
an ingredient that can substitute for Aunt Mary Lou's heart and soul.

SERVES 6 TO 8

FOR THE FILLING

One 6-ounce package Lime
    Jell-O

One 16-ounce tub Cool Whip

Candied lime slices for
    garnish

FOR THE CRUST

1½ cups graham cracker
    crumbs

½ cup cashew pieces

¼ cup (1 stick) butter,
    melted

¼ cup light brown sugar,
    firmly packed

MAKE THE JELL-O according to the box instructions, then set
it in the refrigerator for 2 hours.

WHILE THE JELL-O sets, make the pie crust. Place the graham
cracker crumbs and cashews in the bowl of a food processor and
pulse until the mixture is coarse. Add the butter and brown sugar,
then process on high until the mixture is finely ground.

POUR THE GRAHAM cracker mixture into a deep 9-inch pie
plate or springform pan. Press the mixture firmly into the bottom
and up the sides, then set in the refrigerator for up to 2 hours.

TO ASSEMBLE: REMOVE the Jell-O and crust from the refrigerator. Using a hand mixer, blend the Jell-O with the Cool Whip
until just incorporated so that some pieces of the Jell-O punctuate
the whipped cream. Pour the filling into the pie crust and return
it to the refrigerator for at least 8 hours or overnight. When ready
to serve, garnish with the candied lime slices.

Nana's Sweet Potato Pie

Anytime there was a bake sale at the church, my Nana would get a call. Before the church lady on the other end could even get the question out, Nana would say, "How many pies you need?" Her sweet potato pie looked like stained glass on top—shiny and delicate, like it could just shatter. When she was near 90, I asked her to teach me how to make this pie her way, because mine never came out the same. As I beat the sweet potatoes into submission, she kept telling me to keep going until the puree was as silky as baby food. And then she shared with me her secret: Just before the pie was done, she would take it out of the oven and brush the top with evaporated milk. She'd do it again and again like she was shellacking wood until it had that nice sheen.

SERVES 8

FOR A SINGLE PIE CRUST

2⅔ cups all-purpose flour or gluten-free all-in-one flour

1 teaspoon granulated sugar

1 teaspoon kosher salt

1 cup cold leaf lard, or Crisco shortening

8 tablespoons ice-cold water

FOR THE FILLING

3 large sweet potatoes, about 1½ pounds

2 large eggs

1½ cups granulated sugar

¼ cup (1 stick) unsalted butter, at room temperature

1½ teaspoons ground cinnamon

¼ teaspoon freshly ground nutmeg

One 12-ounce can evaporated milk

PREHEAT THE OVEN to 350°F.

IN A LARGE bowl, sift together the flour, 1 teaspoon sugar, and salt. Cut the lard into the flour using a fork or pastry cutter until the dough resembles a bowl of little field peas.

USING A FORK, mix in 2 tablespoons of the ice water at a time until the dough forms into a smooth ball. Turn the ball out onto a clean kitchen towel or large piece of plastic wrap and flatten it into a ½-inch-thick round. Wrap the round and place it in the refrigerator for half an hour.

AFTER THE DOUGH has chilled, remove it from the refrigerator. Dust a clean surface with a couple tablespoons of all-purpose flour and place the unwrapped dough round on the flour. Dust a rolling pin and roll out the round until it is at least a 12-inch circle to fit a deep-dish pie plate.

LAY THE DOUGH over the pie plate and gently press it into the dish, covering the side. Roll the top edges of the dough under, then using your thumb and forefinger, crimp the edges. Run a paring knife around the edges to trim off any excess. Set the pie crust inside the refrigerator until you are ready to fill and bake.

(CONTINUED)

WASH AND PAT dry the sweet potatoes. Cut them into 1-inch chunks, then boil them until they are knife tender, approximately 20 minutes. Drain the sweet potatoes, then set them aside to cool. Once you can handle them, peel and discard the skin.

IN A MEDIUM mixing bowl, beat together the sweet potatoes, eggs, 1¼ cups of the sugar, butter, 1 teaspoon of the cinnamon, and nutmeg until well combined, approximately 2 to 3 minutes. Add the evaporated milk a little at a time until the filling becomes loose, reserving 1 tablespoon of the liquid. Pour the filling into the prepared pie crust.

HEAT THE REMAINING ¼ cup sugar, ½ teaspoon cinnamon, and 1 tablespoon evaporated milk in a small saucepan over medium heat until the sugar is completely dissolved. Brush the spiced milk mixture across the top of the pie filling.

PLACE THE PIE into the oven and bake for 50 minutes, or until the pie is set and firm to the touch. Remove the pie from the oven and allow it to cool slightly before serving.

TIP: *It's perfectly fine to use a store-bought crust to save time and energy, but if you've got an extra moment, make it from scratch. The old-school pie crust recipe here is simple, and the leaf lard makes the tender crust simultaneously shatter with crispness and melt on your tongue.*

Morning Apple Turnovers with Salted Caramel Sauce

This recipe is an ode to my dad. Even though he's 78 years old now, desserts are still his trade. His specialty is, and always will be, puff pastry. On most days, you could find a mound of laminated dough with a piece of butter on it in our refrigerator just waiting for the next croissant, cheese Danish, or cinnamon roll. When I was thinking what could work for the home cook while trying to emulate my dad and put my own signature on it, I crafted a recipe that evokes a hand pie, something you can sit and savor or carry with you to work or school. You can use whatever fruit is in season— strawberries in the winter, peaches or blueberries in the summer.

SERVES 4 TO 6

FOR THE FILLING

3 Granny Smith apples, peeled, cored, and diced

4 tablespoons Sucanat (see Note on page 194)

1 teaspoon arrowroot or cornstarch

1 teaspoon ground cinnamon

½ teaspoon ground mace

FOR THE PUFF PASTRY

2½ cups all-purpose flour

2 tablespoons brown sugar

1 teaspoon kosher salt

½ cup (1 stick) unsalted butter, cold and cubed

6 to 8 tablespoons ice cold water

FOR THE SALTED CARAMEL SAUCE

1 cup Sucanat (see Note on page 194)

¼ cup reserved apple liquid

¼ cup hot water

¼ cup salted butter

½ cup heavy cream

IN A MEDIUM bowl, mix the apples, Sucanat, arrowroot, cinnamon, and mace together, then place the bowl in the refrigerator.

WHILE THE APPLES steep in the spices, make the pastry. Place the flour, sugar, and salt in the bowl of a food processor and pulse for 30 seconds. Add the butter a few cubes at a time and pulse until the pastry dough is crumbly. With the processor on, add the cold water 1 tablespoon at a time until the dough starts to come together. The dough should be soft and slightly moist, but not sticky.

TURN THE DOUGH out onto a piece of plastic wrap and shape it into a ball. Cover the dough with the plastic wrap, then flatten it with your palm into a disk. Place the dough in the refrigerator for 30 minutes.

PREHEAT THE OVEN to 375°F and line a baking sheet with parchment paper..

LIGHTLY DUST A counter with flour and remove the dough from the refrigerator. Unwrap the dough, then place it on the flour. Sprinkle the top of the dough with a little bit of flour, then roll out the disk to ⅛ to ¼ inch thick. Using a large biscuit cutter, cut 6 to 12 circles, rerolling the dough remnants as needed.

REMOVE THE APPLES from the refrigerator. Strain the liquid and set it aside for the Salted Caramel Sauce. Place a tablespoon of the apple mixture in the center of each dough circle, then fold the circle over into a half moon and crimp the edges with a fork to seal the pastry. With a sharp knife, cut two small slits in the top of the turnover and place it on the prepared baking sheet. Repeat with each turnover.

PLACE THE TURNOVERS in the preheated oven and bake for 20 minutes, until the dough is firm, golden brown, and flaky. Remove the pastries from the oven and allow them to cool for 10 minutes.

MEANWHILE, PREPARE THE Salted Caramel Sauce. In a large saucepan, combine the Sucanat, reserved apple liquid, and water and whisk until the sugar is dissolved. Place the saucepan over medium heat and add the butter. Allow the syrup to come to a boil, stirring constantly until it turns a golden amber color. Be careful not to let it burn.

SLOWLY ADD THE heavy cream and let the sauce boil, making sure the mixture does not bubble over. Remove the sauce from the heat and continue stirring to cool the sauce as it thickens and comes together.

DRIZZLE THE SALTED Caramel Sauce over the turnovers and serve.

Daddy's Old-Fashioned Oatmeal Cookies

My parents divorced when I was between 13 and 14 years old. And missing my dad took the shape and smell of the oatmeal cookies he'd make for us and say, "I'm going to leave these right here." When he made them, it was a thing. Some families had chocolate chip cookies, others had snickerdoodle. Our family's was my dad's oatmeal cookies.

MAKES 4 DOZEN COOKIES

1½ cups all-purpose flour

1 teaspoon baking soda

1 teaspoon ground cinnamon

½ teaspoon kosher salt

1 cup (2 sticks) butter, softened

¾ cup brown sugar, firmly packed

½ cup granulated sugar

2 eggs

1 teaspoon vanilla

3 cups quick or old-fashioned oats

1 cup raisins

PREHEAT THE OVEN to 350°F and line a baking sheet with parchment paper.

IN A LARGE bowl, stir together the flour, baking soda, cinnamon, and salt. Set aside.

IN THE BOWL of a stand mixer on medium speed, beat together the butter and sugars until pale and creamy, approximately 3 minutes.

ADD THE EGGS one at a time, beating well after each one, then add the vanilla. Turn the mixer to low and blend in the flour mixture until well combined. Turn off the mixer and stir in the oats and raisins.

DROP THE DOUGH by rounded tablespoonfuls onto the prepared baking sheet. Bake the cookies for 8 to 10 minutes, or until light golden brown. Remove the cookies from the oven and cool for 1 minute before removing them from the baking sheet to cool on a wire rack. Cool them completely, then store in an airtight container.

Orange Sherbet

When I was making a Coca-Cola brisket, I started looking around for other recipes that included soda as an ingredient. My favorite soda as a kid was a Nehi Orange, so when I came across an orange sherbet recipe, I had to try it. The first two or three times I attempted the recipe, it came out more like a float. Now that I think about it, I believe I lacked patience and didn't let it set properly. So I played around with the recipe and adjusted it, and now it's more like the Dreamsicles we got from the ice cream man. You don't need an expensive ice cream machine to get that taste of summer.

SERVES 12

Two 14-ounce cans
  sweetened condensed
  milk, ice cold

6-pack of 12-ounce bottles
  Nehi Orange, ice cold

COMBINE THE MILK and soda in a large blender and pulse until well incorporated. Pour the sherbet mixture into two 9-by-4-inch loaf pans. Cover the mixture with plastic wrap and press the plastic wrap down until it touches the sherbet and presses out any air. Place the loaf pans in the freezer. Stir the mixture every 2 hours for the next 8 hours. Then allow the sherbet to sit overnight in the freezer.

TIP: *This recipe can easily be halved.*

Molasses and Stone Fruit Gelato with Apple-Lavender Compote

Even though I grew up in the Peach State, I didn't really fall in love with cooking with stone fruits until I moved to California to study at UC Santa Cruz, where they have stone fruit aplenty. I was assigned dessert for one of our meals, so I made a gelato with assorted fruit. But I couldn't help but bring a taste of my home with the molasses.

SERVES 12

1 quart heavy cream

½ pound assorted stone fruit, such as peaches, plums, apricots, and cherries, pitted and cubed

2 cans sweetened condensed milk

½ cup molasses or sorghum syrup

FOR THE APPLE-LAVENDER COMPOTE

6 medium or 4 large apples, peeled, cored, and cubed

2 cups sugar

Juice of 2 large lemons

¼ cup culinary lavender buds

IN A LARGE bowl, whisk or beat the cream until firm peaks form.

IN A SEPARATE bowl, toss together the fruit, condensed milk, and molasses. Gently fold the whipped cream into the fruit mixture until just combined.

POUR THE MOLASSES gelato into two 9-by-4-inch loaf pans. Cover the gelato with plastic wrap and press the plastic wrap down until it touches the gelato and presses out any air. Place the loaf pans in the freezer. Stir the gelato every 2 hours for the next 8 hours. Then allow the gelato to sit overnight in the freezer.

WHILE THE GELATO is freezing, prepare the Apple-Lavender Compote.

IN A LARGE bowl, toss all the ingredients together, cover, and macerate in the refrigerator for 2 to 3 hours.

ONCE THE APPLE compote has rested, pour the mixture and ½ cup water into a medium saucepan. Turn the heat to medium-low and bring it to a slow simmer. Cook it until it takes on the consistency of a syrup, where the liquid coats the back of a spoon

SERVE THE MOLASSES and Stone Fruit Gelato with a scoop of the Apple-Lavender Compote.

(CONTINUED)

Summer Berry Gelato

Substitute 1 pint raspberries, strawberries, blueberries, or a mix of berries for the stone fruit, and eliminate the molasses.

Stone Fruit Compote

Another variation of the compote that's a perfect addition to a cheese plate, as a rub or sauce for meats, or as a sauce on ice cream or pound cake.

MAKES 4 CUPS

4 cups assorted stone fruit, such as peaches, plums, mangoes, and cherries, pitted and cubed

1 cup granulated sugar

¼ cup bourbon whiskey

1 tablespoon arrowroot or cornstarch

1 teaspoon ground nutmeg

COMBINE ALL THE ingredients in a medium saucepan and let them steep at room temperature for 30 minutes. Place the pan on medium heat and allow the compote to come to a boil, stirring constantly until the compote thickens into a syrup. Remove the pan from the heat and transfer the compote to a bowl to cool. Store in an airtight container in the refrigerator for up to 2 weeks.

De Spirits / Spirits

Before Galilee Road was paved in the 1990s, the dirt road off Highway 82 passed a juke joint called the Honeydripper Club. It was once a staple on the storied "Chitlin' Circuit," nightclubs and venues throughout the South and Midwest for African American musicians, dancers, and comedians to perform during the segregated Jim Crow era. The Honeydripper Club was a way-stop between Evans' Rendezvous nightclub, located on American Beach on Amelia Island in Florida, and the places along what was then West Broad Street in Savannah.

The Honeydripper Club was tucked into the woods just off the road, and you could hear music coming out of there all night long. By the time I was coming up, it was pretty much past its prime, but you could still see folk running out of there in the wee hours back to their homes to get ready for services at Spring Hill Baptist Church and Galilee Baptist Church on Sunday mornings. They were just trading one kind of spirit for another.

Bathtub gin or the Holy Ghost—either way, you were moved.

Gin Rickey

You've heard of farm-to-table. Well, Justin Douglas of Simple Man Distillery forges partnerships with small family farmers to handcraft innovative farm-to-glass spirits filled with the soul of Southern terroir. He came to Jovan and me a few years ago about cultivating hibiscus for his gin. Now, to make gin you got to drink a lot of gin, and you can grow real tired of that piney aftertaste. Justin wanted something floral and sweet, so Jovan played around with hibiscus and other botanicals for two years before she found just the right alchemy for a hibiscus tea-like concoction that infuses Simple Man's gin with a whisper of pink and bold, clean flavors. With the lime, this drink is refreshing.

SERVES 4

8 ounces Simple Man Distillery's Gullah Geechee Gin

1 ounce freshly squeezed lime juice

16 ounces soda water

1 lime, thinly sliced into wheels

FILL FOUR HIGHBALL glasses with ice.

IN A COCKTAIL shaker, combine the gin and the fresh lime juice. Shake it like a Polaroid photograph as it develops, then pour the mixture evenly among the four glasses. Top off each glass with the soda water and garnish with lime. Take a sip; now say, "Ahh!"

Pomegranate 'Shine

I was talking to my dad one day and he said, "You know your great-granddaddy Horace had a still out here." Dad was pointing toward the woods on the far west side of the farm. He recalled the time that Horace, who was blind by then, guided him into the dense trees to "show you what we really do out in the woods." When they got to a small clearing, all the menfolk were gathered around a still with the copperworks and all. There may be a piece or two of it still out there in that tangle of leaf and branch, and one day I'll put my snake boots on and go find it. In the meantime, I'll make an homage using the pomegranates and ginger that grow on the farm.

MAKES 2 LITERS

1.75 liter bottle of Everclear grain alcohol

2 pomegranates, cut into ¼-inch chunks with seeds

4 ounces fresh ginger, smashed

1 cup simple syrup

POUR OUT ONE-QUARTER of the Everclear from the bottle into a quart mason jar. Place the pomegranates and ginger into the Everclear bottle.

USING A FUNNEL, pour as much of the reserved Everclear from the mason jar back into the bottle to just below the neck of the bottle. Seal the bottle with the cap, and let it sit in a dark, cool area for 45 days.

POUR THE SIMPLE syrup into the mason jar with the remaining Everclear and seal the mason jar and place it in the same dark cool area.

ON DAY 45, strain the shine into two 1-liter bottles to just below the neck, then top off each liter with the Everclear simple syrup. Place the 'shine back into the dark, cool area for 45 more days.

THE POMEGRANATE 'SHINE will be ready for sipping under the oak tree by then. It packs a powerful punch, so drink responsibly.

Coastal Dreams Spritzer

On those days when you've spent far too much time under a hot sun and you need to regroup and refresh, maybe even cool off from a sunburn, this drink both calms and heals. Jovan's herbal tea, a blend of peppermint, ginger, and orange peel, is the centerpiece.

SERVES 4

1 cup Sage's Larder Coastal Dreams tea

2 ounces coconut rum

½ cup ginger ale

Splash pineapple juice

FILL FOUR COCKTAIL glasses with crushed ice. In a cocktail shaker, combine the tea and rum and gently shake. Pour the mixture among the four glasses, then follow with the ginger ale. Top off each with a splash of pineapple juice. Enjoy!

TIP: *If you cannot get Sage's Larder Coastal Dreams tea, you can brew a mixture of herbal hibiscus, orange spice, and peppermint teas.*

Buttery Scotch

As a kid, I loved those hard butterscotch candies wrapped in the bright yellow cellophane, the kind you could buy by the pound. Now that I'm a little bit older, I like my candy in a highball glass. This drink, with its caramel, is ideal for early spring or late fall.

SERVES 4

4 shots (1½ ounces each) single-malt Scotch or bourbon

4 shots (1½ ounces each) butterscotch schnapps

4 large ice cubes

POUR ONE SHOT each of the Scotch or bourbon and butterscotch schnapps in four highball glasses. Gently stir, then add one large ice cube. Sip and savor.

Hot Rum Toddy

If any of us cousins had a cold or the crud, our moms would call Nana, and she would tell them to send us over. We'd walk the one yard over, and Nana would have her "cure-all" waiting. You'd drink it, walk back home, crawl into bed, and sweat it out. This cuppa cured whatever ailed you. It'll also keep you toasty on a cold winter night—which we do get occasionally down in these parts.

SERVES 2

2 teaspoons local honey

3 ounces Richland Rum

4 tablespoons lime juice

2 cups hot water

PUT 1 TEASPOON honey, 1½ ounces rum, and 2 teaspoons lime juice each into two mugs. Fill the mugs with hot water. Stir until the honey dissolves, then sip slowly and let the warmth wash over you.

Richland Rum

On a 1,700-acre farm just southeast of Columbus, Georgia, Erik and Karin Vonk grow between 150 and 180 acres of Georgia red sugarcane. Their team harvests the annual crop by hand, presses it immediately into a juice, and then boils the juice into pure cane syrup. Some of that syrup is bottled as Almost Rum cane syrup. The majority of it, though, is fermented with a particular strain of yeast. The mash is then distilled in hammered copper pot stills manufactured in and shipped from Portugal. Richland Rum's entire production process takes place in seven repurposed brick buildings along the main street of the town of Richmond, making it the only single-estate rum produced in Georgia.

The Vonks opened their Brunswick, Georgia, outpost in 2018 after the production for the Ben Affleck movie *Live by Night* spruced up some buildings and spurred downtown revitalization efforts. Richland Rum has both a storefront and production facility in a former JCPenney department store on Newcastle Street, where white rum is distilled and aged in toasted oak barrels.

Raiford's Blood and Sand

One day at a local restaurant, I was sitting and sipping, when someone a few seats away overheard that I had been in the military. The kind fellow ordered me a drink and we toasted. This was the drink, and I've been ordering them ever since. Now, who's going to be mad at that?

SERVES 1

1 ounce Monkey Shoulder Scotch

¾ ounce freshly squeezed blood orange juice, no pulp

¾ ounce sweet vermouth

¾ ounce Cherry Heering liqueur

1 slice of orange

IN A COCKTAIL shaker, combine all the ingredients except the orange slice with a handful of ice and shake as the saying goes: if you ain't breaking a sweat, you ain't shaking hard enough.

STRAIN THE LIQUID into a highball glass. Then place the orange slice over the glass. Light a match, hold it over the orange slice to slightly burn the peel and let the oils drip into the drink.

BLOW OUT THE match. Twist the orange and garnish the class. *Salud!*

Boilermaker Times Two

The first time I came home on leave from the military, my dad took me out for a drink. We slipped into one of those speakeasies that wasn't supposed to be open on a Sunday, but everyone knew it was. He ordered us both beers and shots of whiskey, and he showed me how to sip the beer then pour in the shot for dramatic effect. There are many combinations you can try, so I offer two of my favorites. Here's to you, Dad.

SERVES 1

1 pint sour ale

1½ ounces Simple Man Distillery's Vodka

1 pint of Service Brewing Co.'s Compass Rose IPA

1½ ounces Simple Man Distillery's Gullah Geechee Gin

POUR YOUR FAVORITE sour ale in a super-chilled pint glass (I keep mine in the freezer). Pour the vodka in a shot glass. Down the vodka and enjoy the beer as a chaser.

POUR THE IPA into a super-chilled pint glass, then pour the gin into the beer. Take your time and enjoy the vibe.

Service Brewing Co., Savannah, Georgia

Little did Meredith Sutton know that when she gifted her fiancé Kevin Ryan a home-brew kit back in 2013, it would turn into a passion project. One year later, Ryan, a West Point graduate and veteran of the wars in Iraq and Afghanistan, founded Service Brewing Co. along with Sutton and two military veterans. Their repurposed warehouse space now has become one of the premier craft breweries and live music venues in Savannah. The brewery reflects Ryan's military service, from the color scheme and beer names to a blackboard wall that asks visitors, "How do you serve?" A portion of all after-tax sales is donated to veteran service organizations.

A couple years ago, Kevin and Meredith invited me to participate in a six-course beer dinner along with other former military veterans. They sent over a bunch of their beers and left me to my own devices to figure out a menu. From their seasonal Lincoln's Gift Oyster Stout, I crafted a sweet-savory ice cream. And from their Bière de Guard, I made a dark bread that was a perfect partner for the Whipped Feta on page 42.

The Sources

CANE SYRUP

Purple Ribbon Sugarcane cane syrup from Georgia Coastal Gourmet Farms | georgiacoastalgourmetfarms.com

Almost Rum cane syrup | almostrum.com

GEORGIA OYSTERS

E. L. McIntosh & Son Seafood | 912-832-6005

Oyster South | oystersouth.com/farmers

GRAINS

Carolina Gold Rice | ansonmills.com

Jupiter Brown Rice and Purple Rice Grits | congareeandpenn.com

Stone-ground grits | geechieboymill.com

GRASS-FED BEEF

Grassroots Farms | thegrassrootsfarm.com | facebook.com/grassrootsfarmsga

Briar Wood Cattle Farms | facebook.com/briarwoodcattle.farm

Hunter Cattle Co. | huntercattle.com

PECAN OIL

Oliver Farm Artisan Oils | oliverfarm.com

OSSABAW HOG AND OTHER PORK PRODUCTS

Ossabaw Hog: Hickox Family Farm | hickoxfamilyfarm.com

Vidalia Onion Sausage Links: Hunter Cattle Co. | huntercattle.com

PRODUCE

Gilliard Farms | gilliard-farms.com

WayGreen, Inc. | waygreeninc.org

RABBIT

Comfort Farms | stagvetsinc.org

SAPELO ISLAND RED PEAS

Georgia Coastal Gourmet Farms | georgiacoastalgourmetfarms.com

Geechie Boy Mill | geechieboymill.com

SAPELO CLAMS

Sapelo Sea Farms | sapeloseafarms.com

SEASONINGS AND SPICES

Spice is Life | chefarmermatthew.com

Bulk Spices | frontiercoop.com

SPIRITS

Simple Man Distillery | simplemandistillery.com

Richland Rum | richlandrum.com

Service Brewing Co. | servicebrewing.com

Breckenridge Brewery | breckbrew.com

SWEETGRASS BASKETS

Andrea Cayetano |
thecharlestoncitymarket.com |
courtesy of Sonchia Jilek

Henry and Mary Foreman |
courtesy of Dottie Klutz

Jery Bennett Taylor | jerysbaskets.com |
courtesy of Amy Paige Condon

TEAS AND TINCTURES

Sage's Larder | sageslarder.com

WILD GEORGIA SHRIMP AND OASTAL GEORGIA SEAFOOD

Anchored Shrimp Co. | anchoredshrimp.com

City Market, Inc. | citymarketseafood.com

REGIONAL ARTISANS AND VENDORS

CAST IRON

Lodge Cast Iron | lodgemfg.com

DISHES

Claire Parrish Pottery |
claireparrishpottery.com

FLORALS

Everbloom, Inc. | facebook.com/
everbloomsavannah/

NAPKINS

dot & army | dotandarmy.com

OYSTER KNIVES

Carolina Shuckers | carolinashuckers.com

Seafood Hardware | georgiaoysterknife.com

TABLE AND BENCHES

Colas Modern | colasmodern.com

WOOD UTENSILS

Coastal Wood Design |
coastalwooddesign.com

TO LEARN MORE ABOUT THE GULLAH GEECHEE PEOPLE

Geechee Kunda Cultural Arts Center &
Museum | geecheekundaga.com

Geechee Tours, Sapelo Island |
gacoast.com/geecheetours

Gullah Geechee Cultural Heritage Corridor |
gullahgeecheecorridor.org

Historic Harrington School,
St. Simons Island |
ssiheritagecoalition.org/
historic-harrington-school

Mosaic, Jekyll Island Museum |
jekyllisland.com/history/museum

Pinpoint Heritage Museum |
chsgeorgia.org/PHM

TO LEARN MORE ABOUT GEORGIA FOODWAYS

Georgia Grown | georgiagrown.com

Georgia Organics | georgiaorganics.org

Acknowledgments

THE WORDS ON THIS PAGE will never fully express my gratitude to the people who were part of this journey, but I will try to honor them here.

First and foremost, to the elders from Jupiter to Nana: I am here because of your labor, your faith, and your belief in the dream. To Aunt Mary Lou, for always having the kindest words to say to me.

To Chef David Ivey-Soto, for believing that this kid straight out of the military could be a chef and for always reminding me to cook from the heart.

To Kevin Mitchell, CIA alum, you have been my kitchen compadre for more than 20 years. Our weekly conversations have pushed us both to reach higher. Your students at Trident College are as fortunate as I to call you "teacher."

To Chef Vincent Nattress, owner of the Orchard Kitchen on Whidbey Island, who has dug in with me over the years as we've had the difficult and necessary conversations about how we are different, but also the same.

Throughout my life and career, I have been aided and uplifted by some extraordinary women:

"Auntie" Jessica B. Harris has enriched my life and my soul and made sure I always paid attention to the details.

Alice Waters has passed on her wisdom and activism for regenerative agriculture, living wages, looking back, and putting up.

Audries Blake, assistant director for the University of California Santa Cruz's Center for Agroecology and Sustainable Food Systems, has been more than a mentor—she has been a spiritual guide.

Dr. Leni Sorensen handed me Dr. Booker T. Whatley's handbook and changed my life. She and I have shared essential conversations about the necessity and viability of small farms. And how if a farmer is not able to feed his or her family the same food that he or she is growing, then we cannot do justice with our food and there is no preservation.

Miss Amy Roberts and Helen R. Ladson at the Harrington School on St. Simons Island reconnected me to my proud Gullah Geechee history and returned to me a sense of place.

Miss Anita Collins continues to carry the torch for Geechee Kunda and always reminds me to pedal toward the future.

It's no coincidence then that the team surrounding me to shepherd this book from idea into reality is made up of women:

My writing partner, Amy Paige Condon, heard my voice and made sure I met every deadline.

Siobhán Egan and Bevin Valentine Jalbert withstood the heat and the bugs to capture every detail.

Lisa Ekus at The Lisa Ekus Group took a chance and is now one of my most committed champions.

Ann Treistman, Allison Chi, Isabel McCarthy, and the rest of the crew at The Countryman Press, I am indebted to your fidelity to the spirit and vision we had for this book from the beginning.

And finally, and most importantly, to Jovan Sage, my partner and true rock in every way, who makes sure I show up and show out at every point in life.

Index

Page numbers in italics indicate photographs.